The Connected Company

The Connected Company

Streamlining Management For More Sales and Profit

Frank A. Armstrong

Arrowhead Publishing
Lake Arrowhead, CA

Publisher's Cataloging-in-Publication Data
(Provided by Quality Books, Inc.)

Armstrong, Frank A. (Frank Alexander), 1921 –
    The connected company : streamlining management
for more sales and profit / by Frank A. Armstrong.
     1st ed.
     p. cm.
     ISBN: 0-9648563-8-7 (hardcover)
     ISBN: 0-9648563-9-5 (trade pbk.)

    1. Decentralization in management.
    2. Leadership. 3. Organizational effectiveness.
    I. Title.

    HD50.A76 1999   658.4'02
                          QB199-596

Manufactured in the United States of America

10 9 8 7 6 5 4 3 2

Edited by Toby Stein

Designed by Tony Pouncey

Other Books by the Author:

IDEA TRACKING

THE MODERN SALES MANAGER'S SECRET WEAPON

MEMO TO MANAGEMENT

SHUT DOWN THE HOME OFFICE

Dedicated to My Daughter

Christine M. Armstrong

Contents

Contents

Introduction

The Most Profitable
Connection Your Company Can Make

American business was begun, developed, and grew great thanks largely to people with ideas and the will to turn those ideas into facts. The same spirit that pushed the frontier to the Pacific expanded American business to world pre-eminence.

Unfortunately, in today's corporate America, there's less of that spirit than there used to be.

Business has broken through its own old frontiers. A worldwide entrepreneurial possibility has opened up. The market is now everywhere. But to thrive in it, American business needs to recapture the entrepreneurial spirit. The new millennium will be the frontier of our time; to those who approach its opportunities and challenges with vision and with strength, the whole world will be open for American business.

Frank A. Armstrong

That's why I want to recommend to you an addition to your organizational structure, which can, by encouraging individual initiative right in the center of the marketplace, reinvigorate your company and increase your ability to take advantage of every sound opportunity--both here and abroad--to grow your business.

I call it the Connected Company. It is a legally registered company.

> ## THE CONNECTED COMPANY OPERATES SEPARATELY AND INDEPENDENTLY OF THE PARENT COMPANY

It is led by a carefully chosen manager who knows the local market intimately. And that's where the Connected Company is put in place, right in the market. Because that's where the business is: where the potential clients are; and where the connections are made that lead to success. Set up this way, the Connected Company is in position to add sales and profit to the parent company.

Being "well-connected" has always meant knowing the right people. The Connected Company gives this expression a dynamic new meaning. Because what your business needs to grow now, and will find absolutely critical tomorrow, is to be "well-connected"--connected as closely as possible--to the people who are your potential customers in any marketplace you want to enter.

For three reasons:

- First, to turn any population group into your customers, you have to know what they like--and what they are like. To get close to them, you need to be close to them. Right in the market.

- Second, the market is also where the competition is: and the closer an eye you have on what they're doing, the better your chances of beating them.
- Third, the only things you know for sure are the things you know firsthand.

What does all this come down to? To succeed in a new world market, or to improve your position in any market, you have to go into that marketplace and get connected there.

When you establish on-site Connected Companies, you eliminate an enormous portion of corporate bureaucracy--which will save you time, energy and money. This applies to any market, anywhere: Minneapolis or Paris, Sacramento or Singapore. For example, problems crop up in every business, no matter how well run: with a Connected Company in place, no time is lost in pinpointing the problem and solving it.

When you add an on-site Connected Company, you are able to respond to local needs and wants because you have managers right in the market, in position to respond not only to a population's specific taste preferences, but to its preferred ways of doing business.

Being connected to the marketplace, you can gauge when an apparent opportunity is genuine. If it's real, you can grab it before the competition even spots it. New products can be developed and tested right in their intended market. There's nothing in business closer to a sure thing than introducing a new product whose appeal has been proven in that very marketplace.

Being on the spot empowers you to offer exceptional service to your new customers. There's simply no more direct route to growth and profits than customer satisfaction.

But customers aren't a company's only rightful concern. Satisfaction has to start with satisfied employees. And setting up a Connected Company in the marketplace offers employees many benefits, such as a work atmosphere that creates a competitive "team" and financial incentives for achieving excellent results.

With the appropriate allocation of new Connected Companies, everyone profits: the customers, the employees, and the parent company.

Make the most of the information that's in this book and you'll be added to that list. That's a promise.

Chapter **1**

THE CONNECTED COMPANY:

STRUCTURED FOR GROWTH

The first thing to know about a Connected Company is that it is part of a larger company. But on an operating basis it is truly a separate company. *Its purpose is to build sales and profit on its own.* With that goal in mind, the Connected Company has separate offices, a separate leader, separate employees. You may be thinking, "Sounds like just adding another division to me." Not so. This book will introduce you to features and benefits of the Connected Company that distinguish it from any previous way of adding on to a company.

The Connected Company is the most forward-looking and practical way to grow sales and increase profits for the total company. I learned from experience how the

Connected Company can do this – and why it works. I have created five such companies with significant results. The parent company is The Monarch Company of Atlanta, Georgia, a soft drink company with a long-standing record of successful brands, including "Dad's Root Beer," "Moxie," "NuGrape" and other well-known registered soft drinks. Establishing Connected Companies helped Monarch to grow and markedly increased our profits. In this book, I will show you why and how your company can grow through the establishment of Connected Companies.

This essential "connectedness" is built into every aspect of the Connected Company. The company is connected to its customers by physical closeness. The employees are connected to one another by a common effort: meeting sales and profit goals through supplying local customer needs. The Connected Company is connected to the parent company in two major ways: first, by the shared long-range goal of growth and profitability; and, thanks to the rapidity of electronic communication, by management's ongoing oversight of sales and profits.

Let's look first at how the Connected Company links the parent company to its customers. You know that no business thrives without knowing its customers: what they need; what they want; and how what you make fits into their lives. How it suits their tastes. Squares with how they see themselves.

THE BETTER YOU KNOW YOUR CUSTOMERS
— AND POTENTIAL CUSTOMERS —
THE BETTER YOUR CHANCES OF GROWING YOUR
BUSINESS

We're not referring to an "acquaintance" with basic demographics. We're talking about the need for detailed and precise market education. There's only one way to get that: to be where the customers are. That's the first thing the Connected Company does for you. Paying occasional or even regular visits to a particular market doesn't get you what you need. To gain the inside information I'm talking about, you have to be in the marketplace. Situated there.

Establishing a separate company where your customer lives is concrete evidence of your desire to pay close attention to his or her needs and wants. To make sure that your products satisfy local taste and lifestyle. Setting up a Connected Company in the marketplace is a sure sign of the parent company's intention to work together with its customers to provide the product that best meets local preferences.

The way companies are traditionally run, with most of the power at the top and little communication upward, none of this productive – and profitable – interaction is possible. Conventional management style, top to bottom, may still meet the needs of businesses where current customers' wants are more or less uniform and management sees no reason to expand the customer base.

But for most of us, that situation is a luxury whose time has passed. And when entrepreneurial necessity or wisdom dictate expanding your line and your market, it makes sense to consider shaping that expansion in a new way. I'm suggesting that you look at the sheer common sense of adding Connected Companies to your existing organizational structure.

ONE SURE WAY TO EXPAND THE SUCCESS
OF A PARENT COMPANY
IS THROUGH ESTABLISHING A
CONNECTED COMPANY IN EVERY LOCATION
WHERE THERE IS A REAL OPPORTUNITY
FOR NEW GROWTH IN SALES AND PROFIT

How do you determine where to set up a Connected Company? The market itself is the primary source of information. An area that is soft in sales, a site where the competition is hurting you, when you have a new product with great potential but not an ideal marketing situation, a place that may be ripe for development from scratch – all these are situations worth looking into. Detailed in-market investigation is required to be sure there is genuine opportunity there. When the area where you are considering setting up a Connected Company is outside the U.S., your in-market study has to be in even greater depth.

Once you establish a Connected Company in a marketplace, you are positioned to learn everything you need to about that marketplace. When you are near customers and potential customers, when you visit with them and listen to them, they will let you know what you need to do in order to satisfy them. There is simply no better way than being right there to find out what your customers will buy. Which means there is no surer way to beat out the competition.

PRESENCE IN A MARKET IS WHAT ACHIEVES RESULTS

- VOLUME GROWTH
- SUCCESSFUL PRODUCT INNOVATION
- BIGGER PROFITS

Monarch has started and continues to run Connected Companies in five distinct markets. Each has grown and earned a profit – adding to the profitability of the parent company.

The primary source for our decision, all five times, was on-site research. For example, Monarch opened up a separate company in Brazil because extensive in-market study revealed a great opportunity there for a cola other than Coca-Cola. Our Connected Company in Brazil produces a cola equal in every way to Coke: taste tests prove it. Sales offer even firmer proof: Monarch now has a growing share of the cola market in Brazil.

The ability to match product features to marketplace needs is not a matter of will. A company can't just decide to do it. To get a perfect fit from the distance of company headquarters is all but impossible. The strong connection between products and customers is lost in a typical vertical-type organization. Merely opening a separate division will not do the job. It takes knowledge of the marketplace to customize product features to suit the customer who will be using that product.

> A PRODUCT IS ONLY FIRST-RATE
> IF IT FILLS A REAL NEED OR DESIRE
> HELD BY REAL PEOPLE

Monarch's global expansion through five Connected Companies has proved over and over that soft drink flavors have to match – or be adjusted to match – local market tastes. The range in taste appeal from the U.S. to France to Brazil to Japan is considerable. But even if it were slight, for optimum profitability we want each Connected Company to match its products to local needs and preferences. Wouldn't that make sense for your products as well?

With results front and center in everyone's mind, there is little time or inclination for bureaucracy. The very size of the Connected Company is conducive to reducing or even eliminating bureaucracy.

> THE ABSENCE OF BUREAUCRACY SIMPLIFIES THE WAY
> THE CONNECTED COMPANY FUNCTIONS

Instead of trying to please the person to whom one is directly responsible, the ultimate responsibility is to the job: to doing it right. This sense of individual responsibility and pride accounts for much of the success of the Connected Company.

ON-SITE LEADERSHIP
IS ESSENTIAL TO A CONSISTENTLY GOOD OUTCOME

The leader of the Connected Company is the link between the team in the marketplace and top management at headquarters, with a dual charge: he or she is responsible to the parent company as well as for the workers in the Connected Company.

The marketplace is where the manager's work begins. Out in the market, managers can find out exactly where the opportunities exist and what to do about them. It's important to note that this isn't something that can be accomplished once and for all. It is a continuing learning process that involves lots of market face-off and diligent observation of what competitors and customers are doing. Perhaps most productive of all, it requires unhurried ongoing talk with customers and potential customers.

The leader of the Connected Company shares what he learns with headquarters, where that information is funneled to the people who can use it to refine their vision of what the company ought to be doing in the early years of the millennium. (Long term projects tend to stay in the parent company until they are distilled into projects that are best approached on site.)

An able manager knows that what he or she passes along to headquarters is only a small part of the job. Creating and maintaining an optimum work atmosphere is a huge part of the manager's responsibility. That's why choosing the right leader is critical to the Connected Company's success. In Chapter 2, we'll be discussing in detail the manager's role and how to find the right person for the job.

> THE GOAL OF EACH CONNECTED COMPANY IS THE SAME,
> BUT THE WAY TO GET THERE
> HAS TO BE BASED
> ON LOCATION AND THE LOCAL SITUATION

Both headquarters management and Connected Company leaders understand that different marketplaces call for different approaches. The right leader's own attitude virtually guarantees that. Because this manager is not at some remote spot from the work, but right there, seeing each project through side by side with the rest of the Connected Company's employees, he or she sets an example of being open to different approaches. In each Connected Company, depending on its location and customer base, there may be three or four areas for strong profit performance. With the local manager able to concentrate the team's efforts on the areas with the most potential to perform profitably, the chances are excellent that the Connected Company will reach its individual goal in profit growth.

The way the Connected Company is structurally integrated with the parent company has a lot to do with the results produced. The process of success is circular: results are each Connected Company manager's ultimate responsibility; but it's those results – which in turn "result" not only in praise but in raises – that serve as a continual spur to all the people working in that company. In this way, good results beget even better results.

A bonus the Connected Company offers the parent company is speed. The blunt truth: the pace at which most U.S. companies operated in the seventies, eighties, and through much of the nineties is inadequate in today's economy. Any business stuck in that response time is putting itself at risk. Unfortunately, that out-dated rate of movement is integral to a company organized vertically. You may ask: Why not just put a program in place to speed up activities, to speed up decision-making, to speed up programming, to speed up problem-solving – to do everything faster? The answer is that it's all but impossible to accelerate the processing of any activity that's structurally built into an organization. The "goal" of increased speed will not make it happen.

Connectedness can.

You know the expression dear to every realtor, "Location, location, location?" Any business that wants to be in position to grow with the new century would do well to think "location, location, location" – and act on it. One irrefutable reason: simply by virtue of its location, the Connected Company can offer speed of service.

It's obvious, isn't it? When a business is located locally, the wants and needs of customers can be handled much more rapidly.

Certainly, it might be possible to bring in from the outside a product comparable to the locally produced product, but the rapid response possible only by on-the-spot people makes for service that proves to the customer how much his or her satisfaction means to the company.

Nothing better illustrates the strength of the Connected Company than this quick-response capacity. Being on site carries the power to solve a serious problem with a major customer in a timely way: the customer is contacted without delay; the problem is defined quickly; and all necessary hands are applied to the task of finding the right solution fast. Because this effort calls for working so closely with one another, it has the internal benefit of fostering mutual trust among the employees.

SHORT TERM PROJECTS BRING QUICK RESULTS — AND PROFITS.

This is one more double-barreled benefit of the speed possible in an on-site company. As we've mentioned, most projects here are immediate ones. Undertaken without bureaucratic delay, they are completed in good time. That means sales build quickly and profits keep pace. The Connected Company flourishes and the parent company thrives.

As we have seen, closeness is the key to the success of the Connected Company. The parent company can be positioned close to the market. The employees work closely together to do every job well. The customers appreciate that the parent company has come to them. And in this electronic age, the parent company can keep in close touch with the Connected Company whenever that is productive.

Let's look now at the special interaction between the leader and workers in the Connected Company – and what makes their relationship so profitable all around.

Frank A. Armstrong

Chapter 2

THE RIGHT MANAGER
LEADS A WINNING TEAM

In the Connected Company, the employees work as a team managed by the head of the company. Every member of the team shares in the responsibility for making a success of each project "their" company takes on. Some of the projects seem to call for more skills and energy than a normal team of employees would have. Yet the Connected Company team comes through. What accounts for the extra effort that takes?

> THE LEADER OF THE CONNECTED COMPANY
> INJECTS THE CAN-DO SPIRIT
> INTO THE ORGANIZATION

The employees of the Connected Company are not "found gold." They are made of the same mix as the rest of the human race. That means that placing out-size expectations on them is an unreliable managerial style. But an atmosphere that encourages them to expect a lot of themselves can work wonders. Creating that setting is among the main functions of the company manager. It is he or she who develops the atmosphere that can transform good workers into excellent workers, enthusiastic about each of "their" projects and committed to performing well every task needed to finish the job right. It is through the leader's initiative that the push to excel becomes an everyday attitude among the company's employees. Achieving this transformation from the ordinary to the extraordinary is a major reason for the success of the Connected Company.

That's why the selection of the leader for each Connected Company is Job #1 in importance for top management at the parent company. You are looking for more than a presentable person with an adequate resume and good references. You are looking for someone with the skills and the ambition to shape and build a successful new company.

FINDING THE RIGHT PERSON
INVOLVES A RIGOROUS SEARCH PROCESS
IN YOUR PRESENT COMPANY AND BEYOND

If the Connected Company is going to be in the U.S., the

natural – and correct – place to look first for a manager is inside the parent company. When you are starting a Connected Company outside the U.S., make the effort to find the right leader from among the native population.

In either case, the process can take months. You will interview not only each prospect but people he or she has worked for – and with. You will make sure that open-mindedness is among this person's strongest traits. Most important, you will verify by extended discussions and checks that the person has all the qualities needed to lead without bullying: to be at once at the head of the team and a team player. This multi-layered job requires more managerial talent than being a division manager in a big vertical organization.

If you're getting the impression that the process of choosing the person who will lead the Connected Company takes time and trouble, you're right. Because making the wrong choice will guarantee that the company won't produce the results it should. In five selections of leaders for a new Connected Company, I made the right choice in four. I paid heavily for the one mistake. Correcting the problems took time, and rebuilding the company – and our local reputation – also took time. Starting over is always harder than starting. I learned my lesson.

FOR SUPERIOR RESULTS
NOTHING LESS THAN A NATURAL LEADER WILL DO

Once you have completed your intensive research on

where to place the new company, you are in position to undertake the search for the person to lead – and build – it.

I found that the chance to start up a Connected Company is enormously appealing to some people. Typically they are smart, ambitious, hardworking – and well-connected. In Chapter 4, we'll talk about specific techniques you can use to help find the right person for the job.

IN THE CONNECTED COMPANY,
EVERY EMPLOYEE CAN RIGHTFULLY TAKE PRIDE
IN THE RESULTS PRODUCED

It takes strength, alertness, and considerable tact to build a team that knows it has a manager – and one who definitely is the manager. But to sustain morale in a team, it takes equal gifts for constructive criticism where it's needed and unstinting praise when it's deserved. The goal is for every member to know that what he or she does – or does not do – counts.

A good leader does not hoard responsibility: being entrusted with definite responsibilities tends to increase the self-esteem of employees, and creates a work situation in which everyone puts forth his or her best efforts.

Because the result is what counts (rather than pleasing the person on the next rung up, as happens in any company with a bureaucracy), there may be a healthy competitiveness, but there is neither the time nor inclination for internal politicking or back-biting.

The leader's presence ensures that. Because that person

is not at some remove from the work, but right there, seeing each project through side by side with the rest of the Connected Company's employees, he or she sets an example of focusing on the shared goal rather than on counter-productive individual career goals.

The net effect: nothing short of maximum profit performance becomes the goal of every member of the Connected Company.

BEING PART OF THE CONNECTED COMPANY
ENVIRONMENT
FOSTERS POSITIVE RESULTS DAY BY DAY

The work atmosphere in the company produces these results by heightening each employee's sense that his or her individual contribution is vital to the success of the operation. This conviction acts as a powerful incentive: it makes workers give one hundred percent to the current effort of their company. The spirit and drive created in this way virtually cannot be duplicated in an operating division of a typical vertically-organized company.

The sense of personal responsibility that results in product quality is matched by a sense of personal accomplishment.

What's more, the pride employees take in their work is affirmed by the raises and bonuses with which the company confirms that it recognizes their efforts. Being rewarded financially increases even more the employee's awareness of what his or her efforts achieve. Being given an "ownership" percentage in the company helps as well, however small the percentage. As the Connected Company grows, employees see their return grow with it. (See Chapter 5 for more about how rewards result in added profits.)

At the same time as workers are rewarded for their efforts, the decision of top management to grant so much independence to the Connected Company operation pays off appropriately: by increased profits for the parent company. There's no surer sign of a smart business decision.

From the CFO's point of view, the dedication overall of the Connected Company team leads not only to superior products but also enhances the quality of customer relations. Almost inevitably, this combination builds sales and profits. I have myself seen the benefits reaped from well-earned pride among both leaders and workers in Connected Companies on the West Coast, and in the southeastern United States, Mexico City, the southwest, and Brazil.

Establish Connected Companies of your own, and watch these operations, proud of their independence and invested in the quality of what they make, produce both excellent products and excellent profits for your company.

Are you beginning to think Connected Companies may be where the action is? Chapter 3 will prove it to you.

Chapter **3**

POSITIONING YOUR
COMPANY FOR ACTION

Business is never static. Change is always coming at you from some direction.

Consider these business realities.

The pace at which opportunities present themselves is irregular. Can you take timely advantage of them regardless?

Inevitably, problems with customers crop up. Are you positioned to respond to them effectively – and quickly?

Perhaps there are specific areas that have been weak in sales for some time. What are you prepared to do about them?

Have you modified any products to suit the specific needs of local customers? Are your products suited to your customers' current needs?

Have you considered international expansion? Are you prepared to evaluate the benefits and risks accurately?

And what about the competition – are you always reacting to their actions or are you ready to challenge them with strategies of your own?

THE CONNECTED COMPANY
CAN DEAL WITH BOTH CHANCES AND CHALLENGES
BY TAKING THE RIGHT ACTION
IN GOOD TIME

Possibilities that arise and problems with customers are two recurring business situations in which proximity to the marketplace pays off again and again. In both cases, there is no substitute for being on the spot, because that's how you can get the accurate information and take the prompt action that are the keys to success. Having a Connected Company in place means your people can act on any number of issues productively – and without delay.

Primarily, these are here-and-now situations to which the right response, made in good time, amounts to "job accomplished." Long term problems, of course, need to be dealt with over time. But even in these cases, putting a Connected Company in place may be the best way to begin to turn a bad situation around.

One such circumstance might be a weak sales region. Every large organization has high performance areas – and these inexplicable soft areas. Often, they remain unexplained, largely because the precise problem is hard to pinpoint either from the distance of the parent company's headquarters or from the information of even experienced sales reps going in and out of the region. The nub of the difficulty may be very, very tough local sales competition. Or it may be that what you're selling doesn't suit local tastes. Or perhaps a change in local circumstances has changed buying habits there.

Typically, a company organized along traditional lines will attack the problem of weak sales in an area with a spate of fact gathering. Some people may be sent in on a fact-finding mission, but they never get to stay long enough to double-check the answers – or find out if they've gotten the whole answer. These emissaries are not inefficient; they are operating within an inefficient fact-finding system. Pressure is on them to "complete" their on-site work and rush back to headquarters with what they've "determined." What follows are meetings and more meetings, where vital decisions are often based on these incomplete findings. The larger the business the more "research" of this type goes on, and the more decisions are made this way. Unfortunately, as many companies have discovered, this in-and-out approach to investigating a problem area is ineffective.

Establishing a Connected Company may be the most effective way to begin to overcome this particular problem: by introducing stability into a precarious situation.

For Monarch, and for many other corporations, setting up a Connected Company accomplished what years and years of changing sales representatives failed to achieve.

The alternative to putting a Connected Company in

place is to broaden your sales force, having them work out of a local office; but this tactic lacks the strength – and proof of commitment – of the Connected Company.

In addition, especially where the geographical area involved is large and requires extensive travel for little reward, there's little incentive for sales personnel without a support system to continue to approach their selling with vigor. Instead, their initial energy peters out, and eventually they give up altogether. Obviously, for the parent company, having continually to deal with high turnover in a weak market only worsens the situation.

> SETTING UP SHOP
> IN A WEAK MARKET
> IS THE SUREST WAY
> TO GET ALL THE INFORMATION
> NEEDED TO STRENGTHEN SALES

. If the troublesome market is far away from the parent company's headquarters, the only way to find out all the necessary answers is to move into the region. Set up a Connected Company. Find the right person to put in charge. Let him or her analyze the situation from close up. Then let the people in the Connected Company go to work – begin a fresh sales effort.

It's only logical: salespeople need to have support to be willing to remain in a weak sales region until they can make it pay off. Setting up a Connected Company offers them that support, immediately improving their – and your chances – of turning the situation around.

Having established some stability in an area, and figured out how to strengthen the sales soft spots, the Connected Company can go on to produce improved sales and, in time, profit growth long term.

Because the marketplace is the source of all pertinent information, putting your people in there is Step #1. That enables them to meet with customers, current and prospective, both large and small. This is the core of the "research" that does work, and will offer numerous useful guidelines. Sales and financial reports are obviously helpful, too. But what most helps a poor sales region to become profitable is having that concrete company presence there. That and that alone gives you access to the real needs and changing wants of the local customer.

The leader of the Connected Company is able to focus on these needs and the work force, in turn, can get going with the actions required to solve the problems and get past them to producing results.

THE CONNECTED COMPANY MAKES
A GENUINE IMPACT
ON NEW PRODUCT DEVELOPMENT

Presence in the marketplace by a Connected Company provides more useful information toward new product development than any amount of research done thousands of miles away.

The Connected Company is involved in new product development from the outset. The on-site people are in position to evaluate the competition, the market potential, comparative products, and cost and pricing issues.

This approach to working on new products is far different from the conventional way, where separate departments make each of these decisions. In a company organized vertically, product design is handled in one area. Market research is done by a separate division. Another group devises the marketing plan. The costs and profit margins are developed in the financial department. Each of these sectors may be perfectly qualified in its specialty, but there is no opportunity for overall perspective before action is taken.

Having all these aspects undertaken within a Connected Company ensures a more cohesive development plan. All the pertinent factors will be known to those responsible for making the decision on whether – and how – to go ahead with a new product. Having one team see a new product or variation on an existing product through from the initial idea to the finished item is likely to result in a more saleable – therefore, more profitable – product.

A CONNECTED COMPANY
OFFERS YOU OPTIONS
ON HOW BEST
TO CONFRONT THE COMPETITION

The placement of a Connected Company in a region of

aggressive competition can produce results unobtainable from afar. To begin with, the establishment of the new company and the arrival on site of its leader convey a strong message to the competition. You have done more than send a new man into the area: you've made a financial commitment and a commitment of manpower both of which say you mean business.

And you can get business there, no matter how powerful the competition is – if you go about it the right way. For example, in the soft drink industry there is a constant battle to hold market share. In a case where the competition is big, a head-to-head response is often too costly. (Please note that, when we talk about an "area," we may mean an industry segment rather than a physical area.) A much smarter approach is to focus your competition in soft drink areas where there is less competition. There are open areas in mineral water or non-carbonated drinks with fruit content. There are few milk-based chocolate drinks. In all these areas, you can get around the formidable presence of the behemoth to make your mark. The moral: when you go to the barricades against a competitor that's got you out-manned a thousand to one, your smartest strategy is to figure out how to side-step a direct confrontation and instead focus on preparing yourself to carve out your own distinctive niche of the business.

In general, it's plain common sense to stay away from competing with the name strength of a hugely successful competitor. Don't let pride in your company name overwhelm your business sense. Instead, focus on what really matters to the consumer: value and quality. In other words, if you're up against Chiquita, don't try to sell your own brand name bananas. Just sell good bananas at a price that gives the customer good value and you a good profit.

THE CONNECTED COMPANY IS IDEAL FOR INTERNATIONAL EXPANSION

For international expansion, a Connected Company is the soundest way to proceed. The first place it helps is in sales and, given adequate time, it begins to boost the overall profits of the parent company.

The strength of a Connected Company outside the U.S. comes directly from the emphasis on localizing every aspect of your business in the region. Wherever you establish a Connected Company, the fact that you are there full-time, prepared to do business in the language of the local population, in an independent venture led by someone who is native to the area, automatically enhances your credibility. The key is visible commitment to doing business there in a way that respects local customs and tastes.

No international "traveling salesman," however talented, can make up for an on-site, native-born leader. Chapter 13 focuses on the specifics you need to know to make optimum use of a Connected Company for international expansion.

Before Monarch ever established a Connected Company, I had watched with interest the significant growth of ABB Industries. ABB started in Europe and spread to Africa, North America and South America. (See Chapter 9 for full details.) ABB achieved their global growth by establishing in each targeted area a local independent company with local management that had full control of the regional business. Each company was co-owned with ABB, and had local management.

Having witnessed how well ABB's strategy worked, I looked at the strong area for soft drink sales on the west coast and, further afield, in the Pacific, where the possibilities for new brands were beginning to grow. We decided that Sacramento was the best location for soft drink sales on the west coast from Seattle to San Diego. It was also an ideal location to use in developing new sales in the Pacific area including Japan, southeast Asia, Taiwan, the Philippines – perhaps eventually even China. We made the decision to go after those markets aggressively. To position Monarch for business both along our own Pacific coastline and in the Pacific, the local company we established in Sacramento was set up using principles similar to the companies ABB had established successfully in a number of places. And that's how our first Connected Company, West Coast Beverages, Inc., came into being.

One way Monarch added to ABB's ideas was by giving this new company its own name, separate registration in California, and a distinct area for development. For details, see Chapter 11.

Let me just say here that the decision to open a separate yet Connected Company on the west coast was one of the best business decisions we at Monarch have ever taken. Prospects for new sales developed quickly. By the end of the first year, West Coast Beverages was producing a small profit. This profitability has grown substantially over the years.

With the success of our first new company, plans were developed to expand and establish additional Connected Companies in other areas where there was strong soft drink potential. (Whenever you are considering establishing a Connected Company somewhere as a means of adding to sales and profits, the decisive qualification should be strong potential.) Using the criterion of strong potential, Monarch has since opened four additional Connected Companies in areas as far from Monarch's Atlanta headquarters as Mexico and Brazil.

Financial control of them all remains in Atlanta. Each controller has direct and continuous contact with the Financial Director. I will expand on financial control in future chapters. But operating control rests in the hands of the manager of each Connected Company. That's why the importance of choosing the right person for that job cannot be over-emphasized.

In the next chapter, we'll go through the process of selecting a leader for the Connected Company, step by step.

Chapter _4_

FINDING THE LEADERS

A growing number of companies from General Motors and American Express to Norwest Mortgage and Supervalu have discovered that traditional personnel evaluations no longer satisfy their need to find the right person for each job. They are making prospects for many jobs – from top executives on down – take a challenging series of paper-and-pencil tests. They're also having them seen by psychologically trained interviewers.

The firm I have used has a record of being "right" over 90% of the time. (That is better than most personal scores.) There is doubt that any personnel evaluation, using the typical interview process that worked well enough for many decades would come close to this level of accuracy.

We have found this service particularly helpful in selecting CEOs for our Connected Companies.

There is a need to grade upper-echelon job candidates on intangible qualities. Is he creative and entrepreneurial? Can she lead and coach? Can he work in teams? Is he flexible and capable of learning? Does she have passion and a sense of urgency? How will he function under pressure? Most important to us: Will the potential prospect fit the corporate culture?

These tests take a full day. "Companies are getting much more careful about key personnel," Paul R. Ray Jr., chairman of the Association of Executive Search Consultants, told me.

Ten years ago, executives could win a top job simply by having the "right look" and answering enthusiastically such questions as "Why do you want this job?"

Now, many can expect to have their mettle measured with questions and exercises designed to learn how they get things done. They may, for example, have to describe in great detail not one career accomplishment but a significant number, so that a pattern of behavior emerges.

They may also face questions like "Who's the best manager you ever worked for and why?" or "What is your best friend like?" The answers to questions like these, psychologists say, reveal a lot about a candidate's management style – and about his or her potential "fit" in your company.

The reason for the interrogations is clear: so many new hires turn out badly. The sad fact is, about thirty-five percent of recently hired senior executives are judged failures. This datum is from the Center for Creative

Leadership in Greensboro, N.C., which surveyed nearly 500 chief executives. Academic literature cites even higher failure rates for all executives.

> THE COST OF SELECTING THE WRONG
> PERSON FOR A CRITICAL JOB
> HAS NEVER BEEN NEGLIGIBLE.
> GIVEN THE TOUGH REALITIES
> OF TODAY'S BUSINESS WORLD,
> A BAD CHOICE CAN BE DISASTROUS

Recent years of corporate downsizing have slashed away layers of management, thereby increasing the potential damage one bad executive can do. With the pace of change accelerating both in markets and technology, companies want to be able to judge not just how an executive has performed, but how well he or she will perform. "Years ago, employers looked for experience – has a candidate done this before?" says Harold P. Weinstein, executive vice president of Caliper, a personnel testing and consulting firm in Princeton, NJ "But having experience in a job does not guarantee that you can do it in a different environment."

Human-resources experts, while they lack statistical documentation, cite anecdotal evidence suggesting that executive testing and evaluation is gradually growing in popularity. Some top recruiters said that the portion of their clients that want candidates evaluated – even for the chief executive's post – has climbed from a tiny minority a decade ago to as high as thirty percent.

Frank A. Armstrong

WHAT HAS BROUGHT SO MANY EMPLOYERS
AROUND TO TESTING IS A SENSE
OF THE LIMITATIONS INHERENT
IN THE USUAL JOB INTERVIEW

Martin H. Bauman, whose New York executive search firm client list has included Federal Express, Johnson & Johnson and Colgate-Palmolive, tests all key people. Bauman reports that his business is growing at the rate of fifteen percent a year, about three points more than the search-industry average.

With so little information on which to base a decision, "most people hire people they like, rather than the most competent person," said Orv Owens, a psychologist in Snohomish, Washington, who sizes up executive candidates for a number of companies.

Research has shown that "most decision-makers make their hiring decisions in the first five minutes of an interview and spend the rest of the interview rationalizing their choice."

With advice on how to land a better job many people are learning to play the interview game. "People study a few books or tapes, and they interview very well," according to Patricia Ann Capelli, senior vice president for human resources at the Pershing Division of Donaldson, Lufkin & Jenrette Securities corporation and a recent convert to the Caliper testing process.

What more comprehensive testing does is measure not a

36

job candidate's skill as an interviewee, but that person's skills in communications, in analysis and organization, and in his or her attention to detail. Psychologically grounded testing can also gauge management style, as well as personality traits and the sort of motivation which behavioral scientists believe predict performance.

Many companies now want managers with "influencing skills," because old-fashioned command-and-control management has come to be seen as ineffective – certainly in the long run. Experts from Hay McBer, a consulting firm based in Arlington, Virginia, ask questions and rate executives – on a zero-to-five scale – on how well they can calculate in advance the results of their words or actions. Say the goal is encouraging teamwork. A candidate who earns a zero doesn't grasp the situation at all.

In the simplest form, executives who undergo this kind of testing take a written test or series of tests lasting from one hour to two and a half hours. The cost to the company is small.

At the next level, psychologists talk to executives for an hour or more, sometimes more than once. Frequently, they will ask people what they would do in a specific situation and why. They will also ask a question several times in different ways.

A more elaborate form uses written tests and interviews with simulations of real-life situations. An executive might confront an "in basket" test, where he was given an office with twenty-five to thirty letters, files and reports, and told to work through the tasks and the problems they present.

The executive might, for example, find a memo from a marketing manager who wants all salespeople to attend a new-product training session for two days along with an e-mail from the sales manager insisting that his people use that time to be out selling because they are below target for the year. One good response would involve analyzing the new product's impact on revenue to determine whether it would be worth the sales force's time at the moment, possibly proposing written material to cover part of the training, and perhaps suggesting that the training be narrowed to one day.

"Testing has saved us an enormous amount of money," says James L. Clayton, chief executive of Clayton Homes, who a few years ago gave Caliper a test of his own to determine whether the Caliper system worked. Mr. Clayton asked twenty-five of his top-performing employees and twenty-five who were not doing well to take the two-hour exam. When Caliper identified more than ninety percent correctly, Clayton began using the test, along with multiple interviews, to select employees from executive assistants to senior officers. "Now," Clayton says, "we are hiring better people and we are seeing lower turnover."

At Norwest Mortgage, Kathy M. Murphy, an organization manager using McBer's interviewing techniques, said she was hearing feedback from other managers saying this really works.

In a Connected Company many people are in positions where the decisions they make affect the profit situation of the company as a whole. In contrast, a company organized vertically has fewer people making critical decisions. Is this an advantage or a disadvantage? Put another way: Does having more people with the authority to make decisions place the company at greater risk? Our answer:

Not when the benefits are also considered, because the risk can be minimized by selecting carefully the people given such authority.

It's become evident to me that personal interviews for new jobs no longer provide an adequate measure of future success. That makes it especially foolish to rely solely on them when selecting personnel for a Connected Company, and why I am committed to psychological testing in depth.

In this regard, the need to have confidence in the testing service used can't be exaggerated. The longer the record, the deeper the experience, the more impressive the record of service with other clients, the better. Performed by top-flight experts, psychological testing, combined with care in interviewing people, can help avoid costly hiring mistakes and enhance your chances of hiring a winner.

It is smart to classify the characteristics which provide maximum assurance and minimum risk. Keeping them in mind has helped companies make the right choice again and again.

Following is a list of a whole range of possible prospects for a CEO job. The "characters" are deliberately exaggerated to make the appropriate point. There is a need to look beyond the obvious characteristics of each of the characters – to determine what is real.

The great salesperson: He (or she) has a "selling" personality: genuinely likes people; especially likes potential customers; offers excellent service with follow through; has boundless energy; and is impossible to discourage.

The loyalist: Has been with the company for years in a variety of jobs; likes the company, the people, the products;

good all-around operator; has a stable character; and has never thought about leaving.

The supreme optimist: Ready for any project; has an enthusiasm that is contagious; regardless of the problem, he or she takes it on; projects a positive feeling wherever employed, always looking for a better way to do the job.

Knows everything: Drove the teachers crazy in school; has a broad knowledge of many areas; talks and talks – very confident.

The no-limit woman: Thinks "like a man"; tough with men, tougher with women; works relentlessly hard; no limit to her commitment.

The intellectual: Has more than one Ph.D.; uses a scholarly approach to problems; limited tolerance with most people; very confident on all matters.

The purpose of these characterization reference points in the hiring process, as of psychologically-based testing, is to go beyond, far beyond, relying on personal intuition or how a candidate handles being interviewed. When a prospective employee for an important position is under consideration, it helps to call on the expertise of people who have a professional track record for predicting behavior in a new work situation.

Chapter 5

THE MARKETPLACE IS WHERE
EVERYTHING IMPORTANT HAPPENS

THE CONNECTED COMPANY IS *IN THE MARKET*

Close to the customer and to prospective customers, the Connected Company gets the information it needs firsthand – and therefore accurately. When information comes in after traveling up through three or four levels, distortion is likely. For instance, sales people want every report to be upbeat. Without malice – even unconsciously – they may shade the truth. Three or four little shadings in sequence can destroy reality completely. In a company where there isn't on-site leadership, falsely upbeat reports can lead to sales and competitive actions that actually endanger the business.

A core benefit of the Connected Company is the decrease or elimination of distorted information from the field.

THE CONNECTED COMPANY LEADER WORKS CONTINUALLY IN THE MARKETPLACE

The Connected Company leader gains a great deal from time invested on his own (or her own) in the marketplace. The manager's ongoing presence opens sources of information that are simply closed to anyone operating outside the market, allowing that person to make connections he could never form in a group. For productive communication, there is no substitute for one-on-one communication. The ability to ask straightforward questions and get honest responses increases substantially. Information gleaned this way hasn't already been "interpreted"; it isn't "shaded."

Stuck in the home office, the old-style senior executive has almost no firsthand experience of the marketplace. Harry Gray of United Technologies says that the reason his Pratt & Whitney Aircraft division did so well against General Electric's aircraft engine division "was that I showed up in places with customers where I never saw the top management of General Electric."

Consider how different this management approach is

from the home-office-bound outlook of old-style top managers who believe that their job is to control the business without ever leaving headquarters except for an occasional outside meeting.

Harry Gray is truly exceptional because he started in sales, and management people whose careers began in sales or marketing tend to think they of all top executives can most afford to skip going out into the field because they've "seen it all before" and that there's "no need to see it again." These are actual statements from mangers who, having worked in the marketplace in the past, don't want to do it again. In our judgment, that's a self-indulgence with potentially dire consequences.

THE MARKET IS CHANGING AT THIS VERY MOMENT. IT ALWAYS DOES

The rate of change in the marketplace is increasing month by month as a result of the growing impact of overseas competition and more aggressive, sometimes desperate, domestic competition.

Genuine leaders know that, when it comes to the continuing success of their business, what they themselves do has more effect than anything they may say. Most of the leaders of excellent companies have come from operations backgrounds, so they are comfortable with the nuts and bolts of the business and with being out in the field. They use the knowledge acquired in the field to make concrete plans for the future of their business in the ever-smaller, ever-speedier world marketplace.

The core of the Connected Company concept is the willingness of management to find out directly what actual customers are saying about the company, its products, and the competition and be in position to act on that information quickly and effectively. When management goes to the "front," the entire organization benefits because the Connected Company becomes a visible – and powerful – symbol for the entire company. When senior people return from the market, word will spread about how much useful information they've brought back. Other managers will follow their lead. Those who choose to continue to work the way they always have, behind headquarters walls, will become less well informed and, before long, less useful to the company's future. If they fail to change, they will eventually be gone.

Once top management goes out into the marketplace, the character of the organization itself will change. Whether we're talking about a company with only fifteen employees or one with five hundred or more, a new pulse will run through it. If a substantial portion of management's time is spent away from the home office, it won't be necessary to call a meeting or even send a memo to communicate to everyone else that the company's leaders are thinking in Connected Company terms. They may not call it that, but how they're working says all they need to about their conversion to the importance of on-site presence. Their very presence in the marketplace speaks to their conviction that being "connected" to where the business is taking place is vital. It's how they gain firsthand knowledge of the marketplace.

If firsthand knowledge of the marketplace is the key to

business growth today, inadequate knowledge can actually be dangerous to your business. The plain fact is, the more you know about the realities of the marketplace, the less risky your decisions will be. The marketplace is the only place management can get the information it needs to make the best decisions possible in a timely way.

Management sifts through all kinds of messages from the marketplace. Some big; others small (but not necessarily inconsequential). Some to weigh seriously. Some to ignore. When management knows the market personally, management knows what to act on and what to ignore. This lets top management arrive at decisions having at its fingertips the best information available, knowing all the small signals and large signals, and able to distinguish green lights from red, and yellow lights from both. The decision-making benefit is so obvious: When the light is green, you know you can proceed; when it's red, you stop and reconsider your options; and when it's yellow, you bide your time.

What's happening is this: in the marketplace, management begins to think differently about the customer. Given access to he customer's own thinking, what customers really need can be properly considered. This does not mean automatically giving customers what they say they want. It is about being able to factor in what they say to the marketing decision-making process. It's learning how programs can be adjusted to be more responsive to customer needs. There's just no doubt that, in determining what makes sense for sales and profit, knowing what needs to be done to help customers, to keep customers, is essential.

There is also practical value in understanding in depth what competitors are doing. Is the industry leader out to "take it all?" In effect, that's the way most industry leaders think. And act. If that's the case in your business, you better expect the worst and protect your business accordingly.

Once management becomes open to giving appropriate weight to information that comes directly from the marketplace, that openness is likely to lead to an openness in other aspects of company decision-making. What may very well happen is a leveling of the "talking field" when programs and problems are up for discussion, and major actions considered. There will be give and take to a degree never considered before, and the issue under discussion may now be settled by the one person – whoever that is – who knows the market and the customer best.

Opening up the decision-making process in this way is helpful in numerous situations. For example, finding out what the people with field experience think creates the opportunity to give a new product the best possible launching.

CUSTOMERS DEFINE THE OPPORTUNITY FOR EACH CONNECTED COMPANY

When enlightened managers talk about the "real boss," the customer is always who mean. Managers are made smarter every day they spend in direct, personal contact with customers. Once management is thinking – and working – "outside," opportunities will become clear. The customer's thinking, filtered through the experience and expertise of the manager, determines how to "work" these new opportunities so that they result in increased sales and, most important, greater profitability.

CEOs and other company leaders tell me that, when they became more customer responsive, a major change in attitude throughout company ranks followed. Companies such as Nordstrom and Scandinavian Airlines have worked in this direction for years, standing the vertical organization model on its head. Both companies have found substantial profitability in understanding their marketplace and supplying the best support possible to front line employees.

> **Employees need to be empowered to do as much for the company as their experience, expertise, ambition, and good common sense allow**

How does being near the marketplace help key employees accomplish more? It produces a form of productive internal competition. A "winner" in this kind of un-hostile competition can be admired and his achievements even duplicated by some of his co-workers. That means growth twice-over: the growth, often enormous, that the "winner's" own work brings about; and the growth, also often very big, that emulating him or her achieves.

The evidence keeps mounting day by day that it pays to replace the vertical model with an organization that increases responsiveness to the marketplace, service to the

47

customer, and the ability to take the right action quickly.

To refine the vertical organization, however carefully, will not produce the kind of change and growth needed. There is a need to go beyond "fixing" the existing vertical organization. If you're going to change the work environment so that it's more grounded in reality, more open to the marketplace, more aggressive and competitive, you're not going to be able to do it by putting the equivalent of new siding on your company's headquarters.

You're going to have to add strength to the company. You'll have to put in more growth area opportunities than your company has now.

And, perhaps most important of all, you're going to have to give your customers a broader choice in new products.

The most efficient way to construct this new corporate structure is to add self-standing Connected Companies.

Chapter **6**

SHARING THE GAIN
INCREASES THE GAIN

When can dividing something up make it bigger?
When the "something" is the profit that comes out of a
Connected Company.

SHARING THE GAIN IS A VITAL FACTOR
IN THE SUCCESS OF CONNECTED COMPANIES

When you add profit to the pride of doing good work,
you end up with a strong incentive program for employees

to do their best. It's fair to share the gain. It's also smart.

When everyone in a Connected Company is going full force all of the time, the bottom line moves up.

In our experience, sharing the gain is profitable all around for both the parent company and its Connected Companies. This part of the relationship should be formalized. That's why we're including a sample contract whose elements may very well work for your company.

The incentive plan gives the employee a "stake" in the Connected Company while he or she remains employed without actually making the employee a shareholder. The plan affords the participating employee the economic benefits akin to stock ownership while at the same time keeping him or her out of the "board room" of the ultimate owners.

As opposed to stock, the employee is awarded "Units" in the plan which represents a percentage of "Operating Income," as defined in the plan, payable on an annual basis, similar to dividends payable with respect to stock, and a percentage of the "Value" of the Connected Company, as defined in the plan, payable upon the ultimate sale of the Connected Company. Thus, the plan affords the ultimate owners of the Connected Company more flexibility in defining "Operating Income" and "Value" than stock ownership would, thereby allowing the owners to tailor the plan to meet the particular needs of the Connected Company.

While not necessary, a certificate representing the Units can be "issued" to the employee thereby reinforcing in the mind of the employee that he or she has a "piece" of the financial success of the Connected Company. A sample certificate is included in the materials that follow.

The contract can be used in different areas and different states. It can be translated and used in foreign languages. However, it may need to be revised somewhat according to differing laws in foreign countries.

> THE INCENTIVE PLAN IS AN IMPORTANT FACTOR
> IN THE SUCCESS OF THE
> CONNECTED COMPANY.
> THE KEY PEOPLE IN EACH COMPANY
> HAVE AN UNDERSTANDING
> THAT IF PROFITS ARE PRODUCED
> THEY WILL GET A FAIR SHARE

The sample incentive plan that follows can be used by privately-owned or publicly-owned companies. I have used it numerous times. I hope it helps you see exactly why the people in Connected Companies are strongly motivated to make their operations succeed.

THE XYZ CONNECTED COMPANY
APPRECIATION AND INCENTIVE PLAN

1. <u>Purpose</u>.

    The purpose of this Plan is to encourage and reward outstanding performance and to afford employees an opportunity to participate in the future prosperity of the Company by basing executive compensation awards to Participants on increases in the value of the Company.

2. <u>Definition</u>.

    For purposes of this Plan, the terms used shall be defined as follows:

    (a) President means full operating authority.

    (b) Board means Board of Directors of the Company or, alternatively, the committee or person(s) to whom the responsibility to administer the Plan has been delegated.

    (c) Code means the Internal Revenue Code of 1986, as amended, any successor statute and all regulations promulgated thereunder.

Company means The XYZ Connected Company.

(e)   Operating Income means gross annual operating sales, together with any royalties actually received by the Company, minus operating expenses, interest income, and income taxes (including income taxes under Subchapter S of the Code), but without reduction for amortization and depreciation. Operating Income will be calculated by the Company's certified public accounting firm on an annual basis in accordance with generally accepted accounting principles, and such calculation shall be final and binding on the parties hereto.

(f)   Participant means any employee of the Company designated by the Company to participate in this Plan.

(g)   Plan means The XYZ Connected Company

Frank A. Armstrong

Appreciation and Incentive Plan.

(h)   Unit means a measure of interest representing a specified percentage of either (i) the Value or (ii) the Company's annual Operating Income.

3. Awards.

Each Participant shall be awarded his or her Unit(s) at the sole discretion of the Company.

4. Annual Operating Income Participation.

(a)   Employee Participation.
Each Participant will be paid, in addition to all other payable compensation, an annual bonus amount determined by multiplying the Participant's Unit(s) by the Company's Operating Income for the Company's fiscal year.

(b) Termination of Employment.

> Except as provided in subsection (c) below,
> a Participant must be employed on the last
> day of a fiscal year to be eligible for
> payment of a bonus under this Section 4
> with respect to that fiscal year. Termination
> of employment by a Participant after the end
> of a fiscal year, but before payment of
> bonuses with respect to such fiscal year,
> shall not affect eligibility for payment with
> respect to that fiscal year.

(c) Death, Disability or Retirement.

> In the event a Participant's employment with
> the Company terminates during a fiscal year
> of the Company due to the Participant's
> death, disability, or retirement, the
> Participant, or the Participant's
> beneficiary(ies), shall be eligible to receive
> payment of a pro-rated percentage of the
> Participant's annual Operating Income bonus

based on the length of the Participant's employment during the fiscal year.

5. Sale of Stock or Assets.

    (a) Employee Participation.

    The Company shall pay to the Participants an amount equal to each Participant's Unit(s).

    (b) Termination of Employment.

    To be eligible for a bonus under this Section 5, a Participant must be employed by the Company. Payment will be made to Participant, or to Participant's beneficiary(ies), even in the event of the Participant's subsequent death, disability, or retirement before payment of the award.

6. Payment of Awards.

    (a) Operating Income Bonus.

    Subject to the provisions of subsection (d) hereof, an award payable to a Participant under Section 4 shall be payable in the form of a lump sum cash payment. Such an award shall be paid within three (3) months following the calculation of Operating Income; provided, that the Company, in its sole discretion, may elect to defer the payment of an award to one or more Participants for a period up to one (1) year by holding such amounts in a segregated account earning at least normal percent per annum interest.

(b)   Sale Bonus.

An award payable to a Participant under Section 5 shall be distributed in a single lump sum cash payment. This award shall be paid within 3 months after the date on which the sale is effective.

(c)   Contingent or Deferred Payments.

If, upon an Asset Sale or Stock Sale, any of the cash consideration is contingent or deferred, the Company, in its sale discretion, may compute the present value of such consideration for purposes of making the benefit payments required under subsection (b).

(d)   General Restrictions.

To the extent required by the Company's debt service obligations, the Company may extend the time period over which it makes payments due under this Plan.

7.   Withholding Benefit Payments.

Notwithstanding any other provisions of the Plan to the contrary, the Company shall be entitled to withhold from award payments under this Plan such amounts as required by applicable state or Federal law or by the order of any court.

8.   Beneficiary.

Each Participant may designate in writing and deliver to the Company the name and address of the person or persons to whom his or her benefits, if any, under this Plan shall be paid in the event of his or her death. If a deceased Participant has failed to make and deliver such a designation to the Company or if no person so designated survives the Participant, then the Company shall pay Plan benefits then payable, if any, to the Participant's lawful spouse, if then living or, if not then living, equally to the Participant's then living children or, if none survive him or her, to the Participant's estate.

9. Board's Authority.

    The Board shall have the power and authority to make such decisions or equitable adjustments as it deems necessary or appropriate in connection with the management and administration of this Plan. The Board shall from time to time designate employees of the Company as Participants in the Plan and shall determine the Units to be awarded to each such Participant.

10. Limitation on Claim for Benefits.

    Any person who claims a benefit under this Plan shall look solely to the Company for satisfaction of such claim. In no event shall the Board or any director, shareholder, officer, employee, or agent of the Company be liable in its, his, or her individual capacity to any person whomsoever for the payment of a benefit under this Plan. All payments under this Plan shall be made from the Company's general assets, and no person under any circumstances whatsoever shall have a claim for a benefit or payment under this Plan which is superior in any manner whatsoever to an unsecured claim for a payment by a general creditor of the Company.

11. <u>Possible Additional Conditions</u>.

As a condition to participation or continued participation in this Plan or to the payment of a Plan benefit, the Company reserves the right to require a Participant or any person to whom payment may be made to execute such documents and to make such representations as the Company may deem necessary.

12. <u>Not a Contract of Employment</u>.

Participation in this Plan shall not give any person the right to be retained as an employee or, upon the termination of such employment, to have any interest or right or claim as a result of his participation in the Plan other than as expressly provided in this Plan.

13. <u>No Alienation, Assignment or Other Rights</u>. Neither a Participant nor the person designated as his or her beneficiary shall have any right whatsoever to alienate, commute, anticipate, or assign (either at law or in equity) all or any portion of any benefit or payment under this Plan.

14. <u>Amendment and Termination</u>

The Company reserves the right to amend or terminate this Plan from time to time through action of the Board; provided, however, no amendment to or termination of the Plan shall adversely effect (a) an Operating Income bonus provided for in Section 4 hereof that has already accrued with respect to a completed fiscal year of the Company, or (b) a sale bonus provided for in Section 5 hereof if a binding agreement for the sale of the Company has already been entered into.

15. <u>Savings Clause</u>.

   To the extent that any one or more of the provisions of this Plan shall be invalid, illegal, or unenforceable in any respect, the validity, legality, and enforceability of the remaining provisions contained herein shall not in any way be affected or impaired thereby.

16. <u>Headings</u>.

   The section headings herein are for convenience only and shall not be used in interpreting or construing this Plan.

17. <u>Controlling Law</u>.

   This Plan shall be interpreted under the laws of the State of _____ to the extent such laws have not been preempted by any Federal law.

Chapter 7

FINANCIAL CONTROL IS CENTRAL

Three financial elements are essential to the integrity of each Connected Company. The factors are not equal in weight; but together, they represent the right way to do Connected Company business.

The first element is uniform, centralized accounting. It is essential that the people handling this area be experienced.

All the Connected Companies of one parent company should use the same centralized financial control system. Everything has to be computerized and organized so that, when monthly financial reports come out, actual results can be compared to the budgets. Included are sales, gross profit, expenses, operating income, cash flow, and balance sheet reports.

Audits are the second element in maintaining the

integrity of each Connected Company. Each company must undergo a complete audit annually by a qualified independent auditing firm.

These yearly audits, combined with internal monthly reviews, provide a vital check on the financial realities of each Connected Company. Audits also give a company's own accounting people guidance and check points to use in their ongoing evaluations of how each Connected Company is doing. Each CEO receives a message about the importance of precision and accuracy to the financial integrity of the company as a whole.

All of this accounting work may seem obvious – Business 101. But the importance of maintaining financial vigilance increases when there are five or ten or twenty Connected Companies.

People power is the final element of the essential trio. This concerns the CEO and other key executives in each Connected Company. When you couple a carefully run accounting system with annual independent audits, much has been done to maintain control of the businesses. The character and integrity of each Connected Company CEO are very important. The attitude the CEO projects will be reflected in the selection of the other key people in "his – or her – company" and that includes the chief financial officer.

Now let's look more closely at the importance of uniform centralized accounting.

> IT IS IMPERATIVE THAT THE SAME KIND OF
> ACCOUNTING SYSTEM BE USED
> IN EVERY CONNECTED COMPANY

No variations. The same computer program is used by each operating company. Monthly operating statements are produced on time. The cash flow levels are checked. Inventories are checked. Receivables are sorted and checked. Sales levels and gross profit margins are compared to budgets – checked and evaluated. The vital number is operating income.

The operating statement that is prepared monthly for each Connected Company is produced by that company. It is, first, for the use and guidance of each company's own management. Then each company's financial statements are transmitted to the parent company. In this way each Connected Company can keep track of how it is doing, and headquarters is able to know what's happening on an ongoing basis. Further, the CEO and his staff of the parent company will be able to see what the Connected Companies combined are producing in the way of sales and operating income.

A few useful details:

- These reports should be generated in a timely way, preferably by the middle of the month following.
- Quarterly and then semi-annual reports can readily

be generated.

- The uniform system provides a vital check on the financial condition of the company's business in every location.

- The system is used to set guidelines on gross margins, on sales, on expenses, and on operating income.

INDEPENDENT AUDITING BENEFITS THE

WHOLE COMPANY.

The parent company should have auditors review the accounting methods of each Connected Company.

What independent auditing accomplishes:

- gives a clear indication to the President and the other key people in the company that their operation is under control.

- delivers a clear message to the accounting people in each company that they have to be scrupulously accurate.

- provides an opportunity to put all the pieces together in a single review – for the whole company.

Suggested checks by the auditors.

- cash and check-signing processes;
- accounts receivable;
- inventory, inventory turnover and inventory stocks;
- payables are checked and double-checked;
- questions payment rate by major accounts and any overly long receivables.

Typically, auditors do not look for fraud. They check to see if transactions are being recorded accurately and fairly and reported accordingly. This control by parent company management is necessary to minimize and prevent programs that could get out of order.

THE CHARACTER OF LEADERSHIP

While a uniform financial control program and outside auditors help to ensure the integrity of the operation of each of our companies, at the core, integrity depends on the quality and character of the people in each Connected Company.

Each President is responsible for running "his" or "her" Connected Company. The greatest assurance that the leader has what it takes to fulfill this responsibility properly can be achieved by promoting people from inside the company to the top position in each of the Connected Companies. This has a salutary effect on other people in the total company. They see movement upward, with important positions of responsibility and authority given to people who've earned them. They see an opportunity for significant growth for some of the most talented people in the company.

What counts most is the president's character, integrity, and performance record. Since such information is best gleaned by observing a person's work firsthand, this suggests that it is more difficult to bring people in from the outside to operate a Connected Company.

IT IS FAR BETTER TO PROMOTE FROM WITHIN

My experience with Connected Companies confirms this.

It's the right management program that makes it possible for each company to run as separate and autonomous.

"M A S 90" is the computer program that we have used for Monarch's Connected Companies. This is an accounting program by Sage Software, Inc. geared to mid-sized companies. Your auditors or accountants can help you choose a program that fits your company needs.

Using M A S 90 each Connected Company location sets up its own network; but the central office has the ability to access all data at any time via computer linkage.

The program software consists of nine modules:

General Ledger

Accounts Receivable

Accounts Payable

Inventory Management

Sales Order Processing

Purchase Order Processing

Bank Reconciliation

Import Master

Report Master

Through the interaction of these modules, and telecommunication between the various locations, it is possible to manage the company's assets and provide accurate and timely reports for all of management.

Below is a brief description of each module and what it provides:

* <u>Accounts receivable</u>. This module provides an accurate and tightly scheduled recap of all of outstanding

accounts receivable by operation in order to collect monies due in a timely way. This is critical to any company in order to avoid cash flow problems. As mentioned before, with the telecommunication link to each company, it is possible for us at headquarters to review this information with each company at any time. This module is also fully integrated with Sales Order Processing and Inventory Management which makes it possible to manage inventory effectively. In summary, this module improves collections on a corporate-wide level. Which improves cash flow. Which means improved profits.

    * Accounts payable. This module controls cash outflow which is essential to the financial control of the company. The module processes invoices and prints checks, but most importantly it provides accurate and timely data so that financial reports can be compiled which include payables aging and future cash requirements. Here again, as with the other modules, through telecommunication it is possible for management to have access on this data for all companies.

    * Inventory management. One of the most important functions in any company is the control and safeguarding of inventory. Through this module and its integration with the other modules it is possible to control the movement, location, and valuation of the inventory. This system provides timely and accurate data pertaining to the receipt of goods, movement of goods, age of the inventory, and precise valuation of goods. This system provides customers with immediate answers to questions concerning their orders. There is no need to search through mounds of

paperwork for an answer. There is no doubt that enhanced customer service and improved purchasing policies will help improve the bottom line of any company.

* <u>Sales order processing</u>. In addition to enabling the company to maintain accurate information for each customer, this module provides invaluable sales information for management. Gross profit reports, daily recap of sales, customer sales history, and numerous other data are made available through this module. With the integration of this module and Inventory Management, the system provides a complete management mechanism.

* <u>Purchasing order processing</u>. When this module is integrated with Accounts Payable, Inventory Management, and Sales Orders Processing, a fully integrated purchasing system is in place. It provides the ability to have timely and accurate management information readily available for purchasing and receiving activities within the company thereby enabling the company to make smarter purchasing decisions.

* <u>Import master and report master</u>. The Report Master module provides reports for all phases of the company. This module makes it relatively simple to prepare reports in any format to include whatever information is desired. It is possible to create each required report instantaneously. The Import Master has the capability of importing data from other programs such as Lotus or Excel, and can incorporate that data with reports from the financial reporting system.

- <u>General ledger</u>. This module – powerful but easy to use – provides unlimited financial reporting capabilities. It can create a consolidated report using reports from a number of Connected Companies. Here again, through telecommunication, all Connected Companies are able to download daily information to the central office and headquarters is able to maintain central information control for all the Connected Companies.

* <u>Conclusion</u>. Through the integration of all nine modules and communication via computers in each Connected Company, it is possible to control the company's assets, provide the ability to improve profits, and plan for the future. Once the initial phase of setting up the Data Processing System is complete, the addition of a new Connected Company becomes a relatively simple task, with the control functions immediately in place.

My experience has proved that using the three very ordinary measures defined in this chapter plus the nine modules together produce a level of control that will permit the corporation to rest easy with the idea of having so much authority and responsibility spread so far.

Chapter *8*

PLANNING AHEAD

TWO YEARS AT A TIME

The basic premise of this book is to urge management to use personal exposure to the marketplace as the guide to the business. Financial planning should involve a similarly hard-edged method. The days of getting away with fanciful five-year plans are long over. That is a dangerous way to operate. These days you have to use a tougher, smarter method for your financial planning. The two-year business plan is distinctively practical. It includes unique safety features that will help to reduce the surprises from big fluctuations that hurt cash flow and net income.

But before we explore this approach, let s look at how most financial plans are developed.

The five-year financial plan is still widely used despite

the fact that it works only for those companies that have a surging pattern of sales growth, up 15 percent to 20 percent or more each year. The five-year plan works in those situations because the rate of sales growth can compensate for unexpected changes in expenses, the cost of materials, economic changes, new product failures, and all the other things that cannot be planned for with any degree of accuracy.

> ## MOST FIVE-YEAR PLANS
> ## HAVE TO BE REVISED EVERY YEAR

In real life, the actual results rarely match the plan – because, naturally, the first year is almost invariably easier to forecast than those that follow. The inherent difficulties of seeing into the future increase the further ahead you try to look. Who knows what the new product will do; what the competition will come up with; how the economy, commodity costs, industry pricing will behave; or what the effects will be on gross margins. The answer, of course, is no one. Luck – good and bad – affects every aspect of life including five-year plans.

The problem of projecting sales and controlling expenses is a routine part of doing business for most companies. The only businesses that escape are those lucky enough to enjoy endless growth periods. Few companies enjoy such uninterrupted good fortune.

If five-year plans are affected by all these unpredictable forces, what is the answer? One-year plans are too limited.

You have to think further ahead than twelve months if you are running anything bigger than a small grocery store.

Some years ago I ran into an idea that became popular for a time. It was created by a financial executive with Interpublic Inc., a huge, worldwide advertising agency. In keeping with the creative environment of the agency, he called this method the Rolling 12 Plan.

In the Rolling 12 Plan, actual sales are compared to budget each quarter. Then sales for the next twelve months are projected against the quarter just completed. And, of course, expenses and profit for the twelve months are also adjusted. That seems right at first glance because you'd always know exactly where the business is going for any twelve-month period by projecting the most current quarterly results.

The problem with the Rolling 12 Plan is that it keeps everyone in the organization in a constant state of flux. Sales objectives are constantly changing. When sales are off, the business goes into a binge of cost cutting. The Rolling 12 Plan removes set goals from sales and set objectives from expenses and profit. Still, some financial people love the Rolling 12. It always keeps them in what appears to be a secure position. The trouble is that it keeps everyone else in the business in an ambivalent state. The business gets softer and softer. I've seen it happen.

> THE FIVE-YEAR PLAN IS TOO LONG.
> THE ONE-YEAR PLAN IS TOO SHORT.
> THE ROLLING 12 PLAN
> RESULTS IN INSTABILITY.

> THE TWO-YEAR FINANCIAL PLAN
> IS JUST RIGHT FOR THE
> CONNECTED COMPANY.

It works because it looks into the future just far enough but not too far. I have used it successfully in my own businesses, having developed it after years of using the traditional five-year method of financial planning. It was experience that convinced me that a five-year plan could not withstand the unforeseeable elements that inevitably affect any business. Expenses would be planned to support the sales projections, but again and again sales projections fell short, typically because of the natural optimism of salespeople. (Paradoxically, the better the salesperson, the more likely he or she was to be excessively optimistic.) When sales fell short, there followed the arduous process of cutting back expenses to try to hold onto the planned operating income. But the cutback was invariably too late – usually about six months too late. So there went a piece of the planned income. Finally, after years of frustration, I glimpsed the benefit of restricting planning to two-year periods.

Operating expenses in the two-year financial plan are handled differently from the way they are in other plans. The basic idea is that you don't increase expenses just because sales have increased. Specifically, sales growth in a single year should not trigger matching operating expense growth in the next year. Operating expense changes should always lag at least one year behind. This control on expenses can work to the satisfaction of both sales and financial executives. It works because it factors reality into financial planning.

The two-year plan must start from scratch. The first year does use projected sales and projected expenses, but both factors start in a proper relationship. Here's how it works:

Sales are projected for two twelve-month periods. There is some reach. The Connected Company leader can be comfortable being tough about sales objectives in Year One and also in Year Two. The period is short enough to take into account such variables as new products, product line changes, important price changes, commodity costs, economic conditions, new incentive plans, competitive actions and variations in support programs such as advertising.

The Year One sales projection is as detailed as possible, given the experience of the two or three years just completed. Year Two should be just as detailed. The best two-year plans make distinctions only in the projections for each twelve-month period. Because there's only a two-year period involved, the sales projections have a realistic chance to be accurate. And with appropriate pressure on the sales operation, there's a genuine opportunity to perform to the numbers. In brief, a five-year projection is a guessing game, whereas a two-year projection has the potential to be a realistic estimate.

In this as with any plan, management needs to take into account that raw material costs are as important to sales projections as price increases. Both can significantly affect gross profit margins and have an impact on the sales projections in the two years.

Cutting expenses is tough work, and it's no easier when sales are down. In a year when sales have started off below projections, you can't cut expenses after two months – that is usually too early to know how much cutting needs to be done. So you wait for the fifth or sixth month of actual sales to see precisely how much curtailing of expenses is needed. But that is usually too late. The longer you wait, the more accurate the cuts, but the less effective they are in re-balancing outlay and income properly. When cuts are made after six months or more, the savings generally aren't enough to protect projected profits for the year.

The two-year process is continuous. Every two years a new two-year plan is prepared. Assume there is steady sales growth in both years after the two-year system is initiated. For the second year, expenses are not allowed to increase, so profit can increase. There is always another two-year plan ahead. If sales don't increase in Year Two, the company profit is protected. And so it goes with successive two-year financial plans. An increase in profits does not in itself warrant an increase in expenses. In other words, expense increases do not automatically follow sales increases as night follows day.

Of course there always are some operating expenses that increase almost automatically and are beyond the control of the financial plan. Salary increases have to be based on the cost of living – or merit. But increases in the number of sales personnel have to remain level in Year Two. The same for advertising and promotion.

Does this punish sales? Maybe. But when sales projections are not met and expenses have been increased based on a bigger projection, does this punish the company and diminish net income? Of course. The idea is so basic it should be part of Business 101: a company or division whose sales growth is based on projections should only earn the right to spend more money after producing more sales, not before.

> ### THE TWO-YEAR FINANCIAL PLAN WORKS FOR FINANCIAL PLANNING AND WORKS FOR EXPENSE CONTROL

Constant control of gross profit margins, product costs and cash flow are of vital importance to the Connected Company.

Gross profit margins by product and product line are of vital importance to a Connected Company, to its performance, to its direction and to its profit performance. Gross profit must be determined at the inception of new product work. Thinking about P&L is important, but gross profit margin comes before anything else. That is obvious today, and yet plans and products are still developed without early consideration of gross profit margin by the people involved in planning and development – particularly the final decision-makers, top management.

Product development and marketing people must have a full understanding of the gross profit function in all their planning. But they often do not, and top management often has to stop a new project in its tracks because there is not enough gross margin potential. Only about one in ten new products makes it all the way to a profitable life span. The bald fact is that more than half of new product failures are directly related to inadequate gross profit margins.

When awareness of gross profit and P&L penetrates the Connected Company, every expense – no matter how small – becomes important, not because of the actual dollars involved, but also because a flashy business lifestyle for anyone in a Connected Company is jarring. For instance, the size of an executive office has traditionally been a symbol of achievement and power. Not so in the Connected Company. All offices are the same from the start. Some Connected Company leaders have given up having a private office altogether. Instead they do their work, when they're not in the marketplace, in any office that's handy. What will major customers think when the corner office is no more? If it becomes an issue, it doesn't take much to explain, and the explanation invariably produces positive reactions. True leadership comes from the character of the leader, not from the size of his or her office.

There isn't a successful company in the world that isn't excellent at cost control. IBM can tell you down to hundredths of a cent what each piece of wire costs in every single piece of machinery they make. A call on the chairman of McDonald's inevitably ends up in a discussion about some minute detail about cost managing in the fast food business, such as the number of washes you can get before a plastic tray loses its luster and has to be discarded. Top management at Milliken and Co., the largest private textile company in the world, was always surprised to see that, whether it was the personnel specialist or financial controller taking them on the factory floor, their guide would know the operation inside out and could talk knowledgeably about how to increase productivity and profit.

The Connected Company leader needs a similar degree of sensitivity to the details that determine the health of the bottom line. Every subject, every project, must be measured in relation to its impact on gross profit margins, cost controls, and cash flow.

Two-year planning makes this level of information not only available but reliable.

Frank A. Armstrong

Chapter **9**

HOW ABB BUILT A THIRTY BILLION DOLLAR BUSINESS WITH CONNECTED COMPANIES

ABB (Asea, Brown & Boveri) is a giant industrial company, built by a man who thinks big. ABB does business in 140 countries. In North America alone, ABB does $6 billion dollars in sales yearly. The range of the company's products is also large, and includes Power Transmission, Power Distribution, Transportation, Environmental Control, and Financial Services.

Percy Barnevik is the man who built ABB, a business he runs today with the same vision he applied to building it. There is no question that his foresight was the foundation of ABB's enormous success.

The way he grew the company, unit by unit, over the years, holds lessons for companies of any size.

> ## TO GROW ABB, BARNEVIK USED HIS OWN VERSION OF CONNECTED COMPANIES

It's interesting to study Barnevik's philosophy. It is certainly informative to look at how he put it into practice at ABB. And it's inspiring to consider the results achieved.

Under Barnevik's direction, all ABB's connected operating units keep their own profit-and-loss statements and balance sheets. Each company owns its own assets, both liquid and fixed. And they serve their customers directly. Each of these elements is important, but none more than the last.

"Everything changes when there's a real customer yelling at you from the other end of the phone connection," Barnevik says. "Direct attachment to customers transforms each unit into a real business."

That's the core of Percy Barnevik's entrepreneurial philosophy.

And why ABB's organization is in such sharp contrast to the vertical organization typical of so many large companies.

Essential to the vertical structural model is a single source of authority at the very top of the organization. From this pinnacle, company leadership controls the entire organization, passing its decisions downward through middle-management levels from which they are in turn passed down to yet lower levels – all the way to the lowest employees in the company. There is little communication upward. While the word, as it comes down, is adjusted to suit the agendas of various managers, it is not modified by the experience or insights of most of the people through whom its passes.

ABB was formed, and works, entirely differently from the vertical organization. All ABB products are produced not to meet the needs of various levels of management; but, rather, to meet specific market needs.

This core policy has led naturally to a multi-company organization for ABB, in which the marketplace dictates the direction of management decisions.

AT ABB, PRODUCT FEATURES
ARE CUSTOMIZED
TO FIT THE NEEDS
OF A SPECIFIC MARKETPLACE

Barnevik knows that products do not exist in a vacuum, but in relation to a particular marketplace. So at ABB understanding their market position is paramount when decisions are made as to what can be done to improve sales and to make the products more useful.

This information is obtained through the company's connected operating units in its many different markets.

Sune Karlsson, leader of one of the ABB companies in Germany, says, "We are a collection of local businesses with local management and with intense global coordination. We are unique. Local businesses think small and know how to serve specific markets and in the process make money." Mr. Karlsson is suggesting that ABB's success begins with the idea of creating a multitude of product features and moves quickly to matching those product features to customer needs and wants. This is done marketplace by marketplace by marketplace.

Inherent in the idea of producing specialized product features to fulfill the special needs of customers is the opportunity for exceptional service. A really good fit is made between products and customers' needs, with the result that ABB unit's service is appreciated by the local customer.

HERE'S HOW ABB'S ORGANIZATION WORKS

This ability to match product features to marketplace needs is not a matter of will. A company can't just decide to do it. To take product features and customer needs and try to dole them out properly from a central point is all but impossible. The strong connection between products and customers is lost in a typical single vertical-type organization. It takes an intimate knowledge of the marketplace to fit product features to the customers who want those particular features.

The capability of making the match is one of ABB's greatest advantages. Make no mistake about it: the capacity to bring this marketing strategy to fruition is integral to the way ABB is organized. First, products with certain features can be produced in the right number. Second, the product with the right features for a particular market place can reach that precise marketplace in a timely way. And, the customized product sells well because customers recognize that their specific needs are being conscientiously fulfilled.

ANSWERING THE DIFFERENT NEEDS
OF DIFFERENT CUSTOMERS
IS THE KEY TO ABB'S SUCCESS

ABB's ability to be responsive to customers' needs to a unique degree is truly astonishing for a corporation of its size. The credit belongs to ABB's leadership, and especially to Percy Barnevik, for establishing separate operating units – and fostering their independence.

From the very beginning, ABB recognized that there would be, on a market to market basis, different significant product needs which could be met only by establishing a separate unit in each market.

ABB did not become the kind of organization it is overnight. Its current structure evolved step by step. The company leadership established one free-standing unit. It worked. They established another. It worked again. And again – another success. What worked was given the chance to work in other markets – and did. The current form of organization developed incrementally, market by market. The direction became more and more clear, as additional separate companies worked out. ABB now has 1,300 Connected Companies operating productively – each one aimed directly at a particular market and located as close to that marketplace as possible.

Establishing these companies close in to each ABB marketplace, the company was able to understand the subtleties of local laws involving business. Familiarity with the legal ins and outs in any marketplace is the only way to reap every legitimate benefit there and at the same time stay clear of any legal problems.

All of the above might suggest that an enormous staff would be required to manage and keep on track all of these separate ABB units. In fact, the opposite is the case. There is no central staff designated to manage and control and communicate with each of the independent units.

ABB HAS NO TOP LEVEL BUREAUCRACY

The management and control of the 1,300 separate companies is left to the leaders of each one. There is no attempt to manage and direct on a day-in, day-out basis what is done by the president of each company.

In truth, it would be impractical to put in place a central bureaucracy to oversee and manage so many separate operating units. To put it more strongly still: a central bureaucracy would defeat the purpose of this organizational model.

In order to present the whole picture of how ABB operates, it is important not to omit that, despite Barnevik's drive for decentralization, ABB's head does openly seek some "old-fashioned" manufacturing scale economies. This seeming contradiction is largely explained by the atomized structure of European commerce.

In putting the ABB pieces together, mostly by merger, Barnevik frequently ended up with a dozen plants in one industry producing the same low-volume, highly specialized component – each generating minuscule revenues. He attacked this massive overlap with his usual directness: instead of ten plants performing the same small task, you'll now find two or three. Moreover, any one plant (a $15-$30 million operation) will be producing many fewer products than before. In setting up ABB's interconnected companies, Barnevik's motive was marketing efficiency through customer satisfaction; here his goal is production efficiency through honing the number of plants – and workers – needed to make each product.

Early on, ABB took the position that it was essential to remove existing bureaucracies wherever they were encountered. This meant taking action in many cases where a business was acquired by ABB.

BARNEVIK HAS GOTTEN THE
BUSINESS OF REDUCING CENTRAL STAFF
DOWN TO A NEAR-SCIENCE

Breaking up an existing bureaucracy is not a gentle process. ABB does not permit long term phase outs. They simply advise the people in bureaucratic positions that they must either move to another function within ABB or leave the business altogether.

In Finland ABB acquired a company with a central operating staff of 800 people. A couple of years later that staff had been reduced to twenty-five people. The same thing happened in Germany, where a company ABB acquired had 1,600 staff people; in two years, this number was reduced to one hundred. It should be noted that a serious attempt is made by the company to relocate these displaced employees in other positions. In the German case noted above, fortunately most of the people who were in staff functions moved into profit center functions. They continued to be employed by ABB – in jobs that were productive for the company.

At Sweden's Sandvik (carbide cutting tools, etc.) Barnevik discovered a central staff of 2,000. He says he gasped, and in a short space of time reduced it to 200. Barnevik flatly told headquarters staffers that they had three months to find a job in one of the company's line operating units.

"You can't postpone tough decisions by studying them to death," Barnevik said in an interview published in the Harvard Business Review. "You can't permit a 'honeymoon' of small changes over a year or two. A long series of small changes just prolongs the pain....You have to accept a fair share of mistakes, [but] I'd rather be roughly right and fast than exactly right and slow. We apply these principles wherever we go."

He insists the head count in any headquarters activity can be cut by a high percentage in the first year: about 30 percent disappear through attrition and other layoffs;

another 30 percent go to one of the 50-person profit centers; and 30 percent become members of free-standing service centers (often new companies) that perform real work on a competitive basis and bill operating units for it at market prices.

If this attitude seems tough – and it is – there is little doubt that Barnevik is right that the swift cut hurts no more and possibly less than a slow-motion incision.

There has been a human toll, no doubt about it. But cutting bureaucracy wherever Barnevik came face to face with it was necessary to decentralizing ABB. And all in all, decentralization has proved an excellent policy for the company. Thirteen hundred connected units! Think about it. That means that well over a thousand operations are contributing to the profitability of ABB, building sales and customer appreciation – and loyalty.

FOR ABB THE RESULTS ARE GROWTH – AND MORE GROWTH

By setting up these connected units, ABB enhanced its ability in each marketplace to sell products whose features answered the needs of those customers. Through the years, ABB has proved over and over again that the closer products can be brought to the customer's ideal, the more successful the company will be.

The management of each unit has to work close to the marketplace and to the customers. This dual responsibility, as seen by ABB's visionary leadership, is a golden opportunity.

91

Percy Barnevik would be the first to admit that placing management close to customers and, thereby, to product use, is fundamental to ABB's growth.

> THE OPENNESS WITHIN EACH COMPANY
> AND THE LACK OF BUREAUCRACY
> MAXIMIZE EMPLOYEES' CAPACITY
> TO SOLVE PROBLEMS,
> TO SEIZE OPPORTUNITIES,
> AND TO FIND NEW AREAS FOR GROWTH

Each company is required to produce products and build sales and produce profit. That's the job. That's what the manager in each company must do, and that's what the people in each of the companies understand must be done.

A benefit of having an aware work force is that knowing how their job relates to the sales potential and profitability of each product spurs each team to fulfill its potential to the utmost.

Barnevik does more to insure that the employees of each company will do "the job." He supplies a lot of motivation. To him, offering the proper motivation to his people is of enormous importance. He believes that having self-contained units motivates the people in each of them. In a huge company, workers tend to think of themselves as tiny unimportant elements in this remote organization, but in an independent unit, they feel that they are working in their "own" company.

It is important to note that this is not a distinction

without a difference: when employees of any Connected Companies recognize that they are working for "their" company, this perception is based on the reality of the situation. They know that their Connected Company is managed and controlled locally. They know who's running it, and how he or she is running it, and they know how the business is doing on the basis of sales and increased income.

Apply these same considerations to a division in any vertically organized company and you'll see the enormous difference that the Connected Company factor makes. Local managers are accountable. Local goals are realistic – and agreed upon for sales and for profit. There is in any Connected Company the opportunity for open and close communication which is never present in a vertically organized company.

Excellent communications is a significant factor in the success of the ABB plan. There are no large manuals for operating guidance. There is not much paper exchange via memos. Instead, a continual effort is made by everyone to get to the job at hand, to work as team members on the various products, and to produce sales growth for those products among "their" local customers.

Within each company, focus is put on where and how to look for the best profit performance. All of ABB's independent units share this goal, which has been implicitly agreed upon by the 1,300 people who manage the 1,300 companies.

But beyond the shared goal is a vital awareness that different approaches are called for in different marketplaces. In each company, depending on its location and customer base, there may be three or four areas for strong profit performance. Focusing on the areas with the best potential to perform profitably guides the efforts of each company. In particular it guides the manager who has the responsibility of making his or her company reach its particular goals in profit growth.

In each of ABB's companies, emphasis is placed on the need to know the customers and, through knowing them, being able to pinpoint the market opportunities. All of this produces results.

> RESULTS ARE WHAT PROVIDE
> THE MOTIVATION AND THE ENTHUSIASM
> FOR THE PEOPLE
> WORKING IN ABB'S OPERATING UNITS

ABB employs 200,000 people across all of its companies. The openness and fairness they encounter in their workaday situation, and the awareness that they are participating in the profitability of their unit, builds loyalty and commitment to "their company." These employees have a knowledge of sales and sales growth and also of the profitability of the business. They are privy to the details on the balance sheet and the assets of each company.

Each ABB unit owns the assets which are in place in that company. The fact that each company is its own private profit center is critical to making this multiple company organization work so effectively. It is apparent that if the total ABB business were collapsed into a single vertical structure, it would quickly lose the thrust and drive that exist in the current organizational framework.

At some point in the past, serious consideration was given by Barnevik to creating units on a stand-alone <u>legal basis</u>. The legal ramifications and paperwork involved would be very complicated and the idea was shelved.

The cohesiveness, cooperation, and creativity of the workers in ABB's companies are not a result of any bureaucratic control. These winning characteristics emerge from the <u>opportunities</u> given individuals to perform – and be rewarded appropriately.

USING SELF-STANDING COMPANIES TO MAKE A MATCH BETWEEN PRODUCT FEATURES AND CUSTOMER WANTS HAS PROVED TO BE A BUSINESS TRIUMPH FOR ABB

The capacity to make a lot of money in productive independent units has been characteristic of ABB. Local managers know that they can run small businesses more efficiently than large ones. They meet customer needs with more flexibility and they produce products – and profits – more quickly. To be competitive, ABB has emphasized speed of production, and it follows, speed in delivery time. Maximizing production flexibility and focusing on the needs and wants of the customers are related goals. ABB does not attempt to look for overall volume production efficiencies. The local area concept works effectively worldwide and produces profit which reflects the satisfaction of customers.

Speed of service is one of the outstanding characteristics of the organization. Customer wants and needs are handled much more rapidly on a local basis, and this has an inherent value. It might be possible to get from outside a product comparable to the locally produced product, but the service aspect and the time factor and the close customer relations more than override any opportunity to price-shop constantly against products that might be used instead of the ABB locally produced products.

ABB is an outstanding example of the principle of Connected Companies at work. ABB has proven this over many years through growth, profit performance, and stability in the organization. They have created a positive work environment for an enormous number of leaders.

Chapter **10**

MARKETPLACE PRESENCE:
KNOWLEDGE IS POWER

A continuing program of market contacts by a
Connected Company builds incrementally into a significant
force. Long hours and much patience are factors that will
in time be rewarded with dividends. There is real value in
the Connected Company leader going to the market
continuously: to give the marketplace the opportunity for
precise communication about the company, the products,
the competition, the service, the distribution, the pricing –
all of which can influence major decisions by the company.

People in the marketplace will come to realize that the
Connected Company manager really wants to know what is
going on in this market. Potential customers come to
understand that the company "really cares what I think."

Visible management, simply by its presence, tells the market things about the company that truly can't be communicated effectively and forcefully any other way. Visible management tells the market:

> "We are aggressive."
> "We come seeking information."
> "We want to improve what we do."
> "We are open to new ideas."
> "We need your help."
> "We do what others do not do."
> "We want to be the best."

Leaders of mid-sized high-growth companies spend roughly half their time working directly with customers. They know that you can't accept a statement as true simply because it used to be true. It must never be assumed that something has not been altered by the passage of time, by changing tastes, new needs. So the questions executives ask are designed to discover the circumstances now, see what has changed, determine how the change affects what is being offered.

Sometimes what a company thinks is the most important feature of a product (something perceived at headquarters as its "quality") may be unimportant to the customer. Precise current knowledge is needed to exploit market opportunities. Does the business have the knowledge needed to give it leadership in the market?

Anyone who sits in business conferences knows that far too often the emphasis is on agreeing on something, rather than on tearing it apart to find out what is true. Dr. Irving J.

Lee of the Northwestern University business school worked with a variety of businesses as a consultant on matters of internal and external communications. As a result, over an extended period, he sat in on two hundred staff, board and committee meetings.

Lee believes far too much time is spent considering proposals to correct problems that have not been accurately defined. He found much time and energy was spent presenting and listening to solutions, which, once the problems were analyzed, were found to have nothing to do with them.

> THE CONNECTED COMPANY MUST
> KNOW WHAT PEOPLE BUY FROM
> COMPETITORS AND WHY

No hard and fast rule can be used to determine the key factor in a marketplace.

In one of his remarkably discerning epigrams, C.F. Kettering, the automotive inventor and General Motors executive, said, "A man must have a certain amount of intelligent ignorance to get anywhere." From the start, one needs to adopt this "intelligently ignorant" stance. Many experienced managers often try to use yesterday's facts to achieve today's objectives. It must seem pointless to go out to the marketplace when so much is available in written reports and at committee meetings. But that is almost always out-of-date, second-hand information. If they don't go to the marketplace themselves, they cannot understand today's problems and what needs to be done about them today. Facts and key factors are constantly changing. Personal observation may be difficult, but there is no substitute for persevering day by day.

The time has come to restore accuracy to the phrase, "hands-on." This is what a Connected Company is about.

The filtering and interpretation done by managers who are not truly "hands-on" has the potential for distortion. The urge to report what people "want to hear" can override the best of intentions to be realistic. This is the major problem in American business today as it has always been with bureaucratic organizations, only more so because of modern reporting and computer systems. The tendency to stay comfortably at home may be natural but it's also dangerous.

Top executives in a cross-section of American business were surveyed to find out how the executives allocate their managerial time because what they do inevitably affects the rest of the organization. What they do determines how finance, marketing, sales and production managers approach their jobs. Industries covered by the survey included aluminum, appliances, beverages, boats, computers, cosmetics, fashion, food, furniture, liquor, shoes, steel, and supermarket retailing. (A diverse enough base to be reasonably accurate.) The survey went to representative companies selling products and services through every means available to reach the ultimate consumer.

The survey did not directly approach the subject of management style or method. The study accounted for all the time that each executive spent at work during a typical four-week period. No consideration was given to vacation or travel time.

Activity	Weekly hours
Creating and consuming paperwork	20
Staff meetings	15
Committee reports	5
Conventions, trade meetings	2
Public service	2
Out with customers, salespeople, etc.	4
Miscellaneous	<u>12</u>
Total weekly hours	**60**

These top managers work hard, spending long hours at the job. But they are not paid just to work long hours. They are there to get results, and too many of them are spending far too much time "tending the store" when they ought to be tending to the market, to customers, and to competitors.

Too much time is spent in meetings with staff people. Far too many projects are given to committees to work on and to "report back on." Going to conventions and trade meetings is, at best, the softest form of keeping in touch with the business. The same applies to an occasional one-hour plant tour. Public service is fine as long as it is kept to a minimum.

Connected Company leaders must allocate their work time differently. They have to spend a substantial portion of their time finding out the truth about how their business is doing, about how competitive products stack up against their own, about how the salespeople are functioning in the market, about what customers think about the contacts with the company and its products.

Author John le Carré put a button on the whole matter in a comment he made during a BBC television broadcast: "A desk is a dangerous place from which to view the world." He was talking about his philosophy of writing and the sources of his material and inspiration, but he might just as well have been talking about any business. The job of going out to your market, to customers and to competitors is never delegated by the Connected Company leader.

THE CONNECTED COMPANY LEADER LIVES
AND WORKS IN THE MARKET

In the small town of Starkville, Mississippi, a Wal-Mart store stands on a high hill just outside of town. I went into this clean, brightly lit, fully stocked store and asked clerks for help with five different items.

They not only had the answers to my questions but they guided me to the products with apparently genuine interest.

They clearly reflected Wal-Mart's attitude: "We're here to help you any way we can." Unless you've never been to a Wal-Mart, I'm sure you believe that.

This method of gaining information about how a business works that I used in Starkville reflects an indispensable need throughout business to meet and know all the people in the entire chain of production and distribution. These are the people who touch a product or service from origin to ultimate user. All of them know things that can be useful.

In many ways Sam Walton is still with us. He never used an office for anything more than a place to pick up his mail. He built and ran Wal-Mart by being where the business happens.

He always knew what was selling and what was not. And he knew why.

This kind of management is vital for the people in the Connected Company. Managers are the front line when it comes to knowing what they do and how they do it. When employees see that this is the way their Connected Company is being managed, whatever their position, they will be eager to talk and to help.

This is managing in a radically different form and place: it is management away from the office. It involves thinking about the business in the midst of a multitude of stimuli that present realities that executives at headquarters rarely face. That is quite different from thinking about the business in the home office or thinking about the business among staff people or thinking about the business at meetings or thinking about the business while reading reports. It is different from thinking about the people who cannot know firsthand what is happening and why, because they are not there.

This is managing in the most stimulating environment possible. Every contact will produce information about the business. A ten-hour day out in the market with people at all levels produces hours of useful information about the business. More and more management people believe totally in this new method of front-line leadership.

In the past, companies looked for executives who could delegate responsibility and then coach, cajole, or threaten their people to get the job done. Not any more. Nowadays, managers have got to get their hands dirty.

THE CONNECTED COMPANY IS LOCATED
WHERE THE BUSINESS HAPPENS
BY THE PEOPLE WHO MAKE IT HAPPEN

The Connected Company leaders must get away from the whole idea that the office is where the business begins and ends. The Connected Company works in the marketplace and leads from the marketplace. With that orientation, everything else needed to make the business competitive and aggressive and effective will follow.

The best companies today learn from the people they serve. That's how they provide unparalleled quality, service, and reliability. They succeed by being customer-oriented. Many innovative companies got their best product ideas from customers – from listening, intently and regularly. It is a shame that, in many companies, when you give customers special service, it's an exception. That situation isn't possible with a Connected Company.

What all of this suggests is that the organizational chart must almost literally be turned upside down. Nordstrom, the big retailer has done it. There, top management's role is to support the front-line people. This remarkable company manages to operate like a Connected Company despite its larger size.

Take all the evidence together, and a clear picture emerges of the successful company's organization. It will be flatter because it will have fewer layers; and it will have more autonomous units, with more local authority and fewer central-staff second-guessers. Working in the field, the Connected Company leader becomes a magnet for the information needed to build sales in a specific area.

Unfortunately, many top executives delude themselves about how they operate. Consider these comments:

- "My style always has been hands-on. All the office work and paperwork has to be done, but I like to stay close to the market, talk on the phone to every regional manager every week and take every call from important customers at any time." (Auto parts)

- "I try to stay close to the market. It's not easy. Our shares in Cincinnati and Salt Lake and Phoenix and Boston are up for this last period, but we're losing in Chicago, Minneapolis, Oshkosh and Indianapolis. That mid-west region is beginning to worry me.

We lost share overall last year, but I'm tracking it closely." (A marketing director in soap)

- "I started on the street in Des Moines. I'll never forget my first year on a sales route. I don't get out as much as I would like to now, but I still stay in touch with the market. Only last week when I was in Des Moines..." (Sales manager in paper products)

- "I have every major competitive model in my house, nine of them. I like to see how they perform against our newest models. I project to the consumer, I see what they see. See what they like. It's a rather simple method and for me, it works." (Television)

- "You know this is one tough business. The whole thing starts all over every season. I have my girls constantly shopping every competitor. Not only here. But in Los Angeles, Dallas and Miami. A bit tricky, but we get it done. In this business you stay close to the customer, or you drop dead." (Fashion)

Each of these executives believes it is essential to stay close to the market, close to the customer, close to the competition. But none of them does it. They talk about being "hands-on," about being close to the market, but as you read their comments you see that while they talk the talk, they fail to walk the walk.

And, in order to stay healthy, you need to do some

serious walking. That way, when you get down to talking – and listening – you'll be where the business is. In the marketplace.

Frank A. Armstrong

Chapter **11**

MOVING AHEAD IN AN
EVER-FASTER WORLD

Monarch's home base is Atlanta. We'd been doing some business out west. We saw an opportunity to do more in that marketplace. Looking at the potential, we concluded that if we were going to build our business there, we would have to commit to establishing a company in California that could attract and service customers in the entire Pacific area.

This conclusion led to establishing a Connected Company there. One of our best managers was put in charge to work the market day-in and day-out. The sheer presence of the manager produced some initial results. The business grew. Why? Because it was there, close at hand, capable of following up every prospect, ready to service customers, and able to convince new customers that the service would be good all of the time.

Putting the right person in as leader was very important. Equally important was providing him with the incentive and appropriate return for making the business grow.

The customer base has to be evaluated and measured in terms of the different sales potentials and margin potentials. This potential can be seen once you have broken down your customer groups, and looked at each as a distinct marketplace. In the USA, variations in the character and bias of various regions are becoming more precisely defined year by year.

AS COMPETITION INCREASES IN
INDUSTRY AFTER INDUSTRY,
THERE IS A NEED FOR GREATER SPEED
IN MAKING DECISIONS AND TAKING ACTIONS

Elaborate programs for launching and testing new products are now condensed significantly. In the past, it was popular – and often productive – to use multiple comparative markets for test marketing. Today, a plan that complex simply doesn't produce fast enough answers.

The tempo of competition in most industries has accelerated to a degree that prohibits elaborate planning, exhaustive fact-gathering, leisurely evaluation, and – finally – decision-making. The right decision, arrived at too slowly, becomes useless.

The rate of movement built into the vertical organization has become out-dated. Any business that continues to operate at that pace puts itself at risk.

You may ask: Why not just put a program in place in the vertical organization to speed up activities, to speed up decision making, to speed up programming – to speed up the way everything is done in the company? The sad answer is that it's hard to accelerate the processing of any activity in a typical vertical operation.

To get more speed in a business, the best way is to set up Connected Companies. These companies provide the mechanism that produces the fastest kind of decision making. Programs are defined quickly. And closeness to the action produces a condition in which judgments come faster – and have a good chance to be more accurate.

"I've got the problem. I understand it. I'll get back to you right away." When said by someone at the helm in a Connected Company, "right away" is the same day or at most the day after. This quick-response capacity is reason enough to look seriously at setting up Connected Companies in specifically defined markets.

Connected Companies have a tempo that is needed by successful businesses today. Entrepreneurial companies do not have the luxury of deliberating a long time over every major decision.

CONNECTED COMPANIES CAN CORRECT PROBLEM AREAS

Problem areas can be corrected or at least minimized by putting in place a Connected Company with the specific mandate to attack the problem.

111

Here are some examples of what a Connected Company can achieve.

Decrease new product failures. Every company has its share. The job is to improve the ratio of successes to failures, and thereby give the whole process a more positive result. This can happen with the Connected Company because, with the department-by-department set-up gone, a focused team of people – with focused energy and focused talent – apply themselves to any problem.

Fix the weakened product line. This may be a line of products that's been around for a long time. Maybe too long. Regardless, the product line needs a new look, a new feature, an expanded use, some specific refinements. This can happen when the job is assigned to the Connected Company. Because everyone on the team knows that if, as a team, they come up with the answers, all of them will benefit.

Correct weaknesses in specific markets. Setting up a Connected Company in another country can help turn negative performance into positive results in sales and profit. Monarch learned this in Mexico.

The way the problem-solving process works in a Connected Company does more than solve problems quickly and well. The focus on customers by the people in Connected Companies is a basic factor. There is a need to know where the customer stands. Not in days or weeks, but now. Because more and more leaders are working out of the office, the leads come from the marketplace. It is then that a big change can take place. Other changes will automatically follow, all the changes that are necessary to make the business more responsive. More competitive. More aggressive. More effective.

And more profitable.

Most successful Japanese consumer electronics companies have always sent their product-design engineers around the world for about six months each year to study the latest customer needs and survey the competitive scene. They visit customers and dealers. They attend trade shows. They hold regional product conferences with dealers and salesmen. And as we know, they have a high ratio of success in product innovations.

A Hewlett Packard engineer in integrated circuits said he spent almost all of his time working on applications on out-of-town-user premises rather than in his own laboratory.

Perhaps the biggest change of all for manufacturing engineering is getting used to the idea that the best way to make a contribution is found in the marketplace and on the factory floor, not in the equipment manufacturers' catalogs. The manufacturing engineer must spend time with equipment sales representatives, but should spend more with machine operators, set-up crews, maintenance technicians and supervisors.

Allied-Signal knows that the level of basic research in this country is far more advanced and productive than anywhere else. Unfortunately, scientific leadership doesn't always produce the gain intended. In the ceramics industry, for example, U.S. firms have worked to reduce the grain size of ceramic powders. And they have succeeded. They are concerned about the esoteric considerations of grain size in ceramics. They know what is needed to stand up under long periods of pounding and high heat.

But, the Japanese focus on improved product design. They do this more efficiently than the highly skilled U.S. product developers who spend too much time in the laboratory, and not enough time working in the front lines.

When the mind of the product developer is open to the front line and responds to it, the result will be far more new product successes than failures.

TECHNOLOGY MAKES POSSIBLE THE INSTANT TRANSMISSION OF ALL PERTINENT INFORMATION

Is instant communication worth all that much?

It's worth everything!

Because with skilled managers in the marketplace, there is always two-way communication with the company leadership. They get the message out, accurately and quickly. On the other end, there's the capability for immediate response. What needs to be done gets done right away.

The existence of a Connected Company allows for open communication among company people at all levels – from the stock room clerk to the national sales manager – on almost any subject at any time. With instant communication readily available, internal memorandums are kept to a minimum. When someone has a problem or a need it is discussed on the spot. And can be solved without the delay inherent in vertical organizations. When there is the need for action or for change, it is addressed face-to-face and a decision made. The same process takes place when a mistake is made; with open and direct discussion, a mistake can usually be corrected quickly, so neither the error nor bad feelings is given a chance to grow.

Do not think that this productive situation can become a reality immediately. It develops over time as people come to understand that management wants – seeks! – such open communication. When new people join the company, they sometimes find such open lines of communication unusual enough to make them hesitant to take advantage of them – but not for long.

One thing a company newcomer is likely to appreciate right away is that in the Connected Company everyone's part in the interlocking operation is seen to be important. Such recognition has a very beneficial effect on employee morale.

High morale contributes to the overall quality of the company's work. In the Connected Company, an individual's complaints are addressed directly; often this allows for a quick resolution of problems. The importance of this goes beyond keeping any individual employee content: in this type of business environment the quality of work can never be allowed to be less than excellent. When someone is not happy, his or her work is likely to show it. So management has a business reason as well as a diplomatic one to respond reasonably and quickly to the reasonable complaints of employees.

Company spirit is another facet of company morale. And company spirit is fostered in the Connected Company because everyone sees that management is working as hard as anyone else. If it's apparent that management works until a job is done, the fact that the company expects all employees to do the same is viewed as fair.

No doubt about it, the managers of Connected Companies work hard, harder than do managers in most companies organized vertically. But for good reason! The Connected Company is a growing company. High among the benefits that growth provides is job security for the Connected Company team.

Chapter *12*

WHY TEAMWORK WORKS

New product development, where teamwork can make a critical difference, fits naturally into a Connected Company. This is especially true when a business depends on continually coming up with new products. In this kind of company, new product development is not a "sometime thing"; it is a never-ending search. In a very real sense, for such a company, new products are the business. And that makes the quality of new products vital.

In a Connected Company, new product team members are aware that their job does not end when the new product has been developed. The Connected Company can be given an assignment for a new product with the understanding that the members will eventually produce, distribute, and market the product in a focused way to effect optimum sales and profits.

As a result, inside the Connected Company, a new product team of specialists is put in place. Its members are usually grouped physically as far as work space is concerned, so that their capacity to communicate with one another is maximized. This has a stimulating effect as they work cooperatively on developing a new product, with everyone aware that the goal of the new product team is to contribute to the long-term growth of the Connected Company.

NEW PRODUCTS WORK BENEFITS FROM BEING IN A CONNECTED COMPANY

The right mix of people is necessary for success: creative people, technical people, production people, financial people, sales people.

Moreover, because the Connected Company itself depends on focused effort to achieve growth as expeditiously as possible, the importance of a timetable is clearly recognized. The time issue needs to be taken seriously by all the workers and balanced against the need to create a successful product.

These are practical reasons for putting a new product team within a Connected Company. The company will help them do their work efficiently, and they will help the total company by creating new products to grow the business.

From the outset, everyone knows that the new product team is potentially a new business. The new product team and the workers in the Connected Company will share an attitude and a drive for results that cannot be achieved in a larger compartmentalized organization.

The leader of the Connected Company in which a new product project is placed has the job of putting together the various talents needed to produce and launch what the team develops. This leader may have a marketing background or a sales background or a pure technical background. No matter, in this context his or her job is that of coordination. There will be technical people involved with the creation and design of products. There should be production people who understand exactly what will be required in production. There will be marketing people who will have the responsibility for any packaging required by the new product. The point is that, if the leader of the Connected Company is effective, all of these talents will work together in the same organization and in the same location, confidently and productively exchanging information and ideas. Facilitating the various elements of the development and decision-making process in this way greatly improves the chances of successful new product development.

It is vital to include in the mix of people a key financial person, with the job of evaluating costs from the very beginning: costs of materials, costs of production, costs of packaging – the cost of every element. Very early on, a skilled financial person will be able to put a fix on the projected product cost and add the right level of gross profit margin to ensure the new product's profitability. (When new products are produced in the department-by-department method typical in vertical corporations, one of the most common pitfalls in the process is not having financial people involved from the beginning.)

Many new products developed are not subjected to financial decisions early enough. The goal is to avoid coming up with a new product that is wonderful except for the small flaw that it's simply too expensive to produce and still make a profit. If the product is priced out of range in the particular product category then all the effort that went into developing it is in fact wasted. Therefore, the importance of having an able financial person involved from the outset cannot be overstated.

PROJECT TEAMS REPRESENT A FIRST STEP
TOWARD SETTING UP CONNECTED
COMPANIES
FOR NEW PRODUCT WORK

Even when a corporation does not have Connected Companies as a "natural habitat" for a new product team, a team approach can be used successfully for product development. For an excellent example, let's look at how Ingersoll-Rand came up with a new product, specifically a grinder.

For many years the traditional split-discipline system was used at Ingersoll-Rand to develop new products. It was the sales department's responsibility to feed the customers information through the marketing department. Marketing was responsible for translating that information into some approximation of engineering terms and move it on to the engineering department. The engineering department then put designs on paper. Then began the responsibility of the manufacturing arm to convert the designs into hardware. And so on.

The biggest weakness in this situation was the series of organizational barriers against which each department's "manhood" was tested. In order to maintain its authority, each discipline had to have a say and that had to be translated into hard numbers to isolate financially the development of a product. At the same time, cost factors related to the new product were factored into the program from the very beginning.

The biggest need at Ingersoll-Rand in this connection was to have enough understanding in the customer group as to what was needed in the way of a new grinder. Eventually, they did develop the grinder – using all the separate disciplines on a piecemeal basis, from marketing, sales, product design, production, to most important, finance.

A number of other Ingersoll-Rand projects have been given over to a new team process, and there is a growing sense in the company that it is safe to embrace this "new way" of working together toward a common goal. And there are currently a number of teams to deal with all long range product development.

Other major companies have used new product teams to good effect. Semco, Volvo and Steelcase in particular have been successful at it. However, currently the use of unified new product teams is more common in theory than in practice.

One reason for the scarcity of new product teams is CEOs schooled in the old theory of "individualism" are not quick to empower project teams. There are formidable barriers to the idea of using project teams, especially where there is a large and long-established bureaucracy.

At the beginning of this chapter, I referred to the fact that, for some companies, the need to create new products is constant. Hallmark is that kind of company.

This four billion dollar corporation is well up among the Forbes Magazine list of the largest private companies. Hallmark has products which are produced in twenty different languages and are distributed in more than a hundred countries around the world. It has 21,000 full-time employees and 15,000 part-time employees. There are 5,700 employees in the Kansas City headquarters alone.

The key to the Hallmark business is, of course, the large creative staff. Almost a thousand people are involved in the creation of Hallmark's products. These artists, designers, writers, editors, and photographers produce about 21,000 different cards each year. Hallmark also has 50,000 stock number cards – cards which are always in stock, always available.

In the early nineties, Hallmark developed project teams, grouping various talents from assorted disciplines, departments, and work places to work on a single project. The objective was to stimulate creativity and end the "throw it over the wall, it's their problem" attitude that resulted from the step-by-step departmental approach which had been used for years and years.

Hallmark's project team program worked so well that half the line which hit stores that year was eight months ahead of schedule. Admittedly, Hallmark did load up retailer inventories ahead of each season. But, the result in added sales compensated for the added inventories of retailers. The retailers always have seasonal cards in adequate volume ahead of time.

The initial success of new card development by project teams put development for seasonal products (about 40% of Hallmark's business) on schedules of far less than a year. Forming the project team made it possible to get a more focused effort on a particular group of designs and cards. There was more direct communication between the various disciplines. The most rewarding experience was for artists and writers to see their work in final form much faster than in the past. This produced some highly enthusiastic support for project teamwork.

In much the same way as does the Connected Company, the integrated project teams at Hallmark effectively review their own work. They start out knowing that management is in favor of what they are doing and understand that management will see it produced in the end. The team is not required to undergo interim reviews by management. As a result, the whole process works much faster.

As the business process is accelerated, people understand that they are not being asked to cut back on quality but instead simply to increase their rate of productivity. Hallmark has been able to get a new line of greeting cards from concept to market much faster. In the past this has taken two to three years and in the process costly revisions of designs and lettering and printing were slowing the process. By using the teams, Hallmark has been able to get products on the shelves months faster. The window of sales opportunities can shut quickly in the card business and Hallmark has taken on the use of project teams to overcome this particular situation.

Hallmark, because of its ability to get completely new products to the market in less than a year, can produce products and promotional programs that are consistently approved by buyers and retailers. And, in the process, they have reduced costs while making improvements in quality. It all boiled down to radically improving performance at the retail level for long-standing Hallmark specialty stores. Department stores, supermarkets, pharmacies and other outlets also have been pleased by this speedup and by the increased flow of new products.

The use of project teams produced a real breakthrough for Hallmark. They didn't realize how much inefficiency there was in the system which had evolved over many, many years. The key factor was the use of historically defined time to get new cards out. There was always time to refine and do something over if needed to make it right. In the lengthy product development cycle, the majority of the time wasn't spent in printing and production. Two-thirds of the cycle was spent in developing the plan and the concept and the creative work.

As to who benefits most from these changes, Hallmark's direct and indirect customers (retailers and the public) benefit a lot; but Hallmark's own employees may reap the greatest benefit. Thirty percent of Hallmark's shares are owned by employees. When the business does well, so do they. And they know it: witness their commitment and the way they work to produce "the very best."

NEW PRODUCT SUCCESSES COME
DIRECTLY FROM INVOLVEMENT WITH THE
MARKET AND AN INTENSE KNOWLEDGE OF
COMPETITIVE PRODUCTS

New product development starts in the street and in stores. It then moves to the design rooms for refinement and improvement.

In a sophisticated product development arena such as Silicon Valley, this type of approach often meets with disdain. Here is a typical attitude: "What can I possibly learn out there talking to people who can't begin to understand what I'm about, much less understand what I say?"

Regis McKenna, a renowned consultant to Silicon Valley companies, believes that every marketing person should be on the road a lot of the time to get that sixth sense that comes only from the marketplace. McKenna believes that, in this era of electronic communications, personal interaction is becoming more important than ever. He's right.

A study was done in the electronics industry on 150 products. Half worked. Half failed. The report states that "unsuccessful products were often technological marvels that received technical excellence awards and were written up in prestigious journals." Too much exotic technology at far too high a price is the story of virtually every one of the product failures. In contrast, the successful products almost always had been exposed to customer evaluations and recommendations.

125

> FROM THE START, PRODUCT COST AND
> PRODUCT PROFIT MUST BE A VITAL PART OF
> NEW PRODUCT DEVELOPMENT...
> BUT HALF THE TIME THIS IS NOT THE CASE

New product work starts by going to the market first...
and then again.

Chapter 13

THE MARKETPLACE TELLS YOU
HOW TO GROW YOUR BUSINESS

The world market continues to expand at a rapid pace. There are opportunities for growth country by country. Regardless of the opportunities for growth in the USA, there can be greater opportunities overseas.

The Vertical Organization has proved to be less than adequate for successful global expansion. An international operation *dominated* and *controlled* by a USA office is losing favor.

Let's look at why this is so. To start with, when it comes to doing business internationally, much time is wasted in a corporation organized vertically. The "home office" approach for the various disciplines involved is cumbersome: using key people to travel the world from country to country. Managing an international business this way is out-dated.

IBM originally did a fine job of developing international markets. Now IBM is looking closely at making possible changes in the way they develop and expand their international markets, using the ABB program as their model. The management of both companies have met together on numerous occasions in recent years. IBM has examined the ABB structure in depth and found many aspects of it appealing. What they like in particular is the idea of being very lean at the head office level, with that office becoming more of a holding company and the main thrust of international development being shifted to individual markets. Another likely outcome of IBM's probe is to make those markets much more independent, flexible, and aggressive in developing business.

Like IBM, other large corporations are searching for ways to optimize their ability to coordinate their global operations. Central to this process is building local strength in each market.

Professor C.K. Prahalad, who teaches corporate strategy in international business at the University of Michigan, has recognized the changes which are taking place. He says, "Companies are seeing that, at the senior level, they don't necessarily need a large staff to best manage the mix of global and local operations. Coordination has a strategic growth but it also has an organization cost, so the essential thing is to find the best balance between central management and local area management."

The Europeans have long been ahead of most USA companies in international expansion. More so than many

American or, for that matter, Japanese companies, Europeans are often comfortable in international situations. The better-run companies, like Nestle, have corporate boards which closely resemble the membership of the U.N. Security Council.

Paul Strebel, a professor of international management development in Switzerland says, "Our cultural diversity in Switzerland is a huge asset." Adds Roland Berger, head of Germany's Roland & Berger consulting firm: "Europeans are better equipped for globalization."

> THERE IS A GROWING MOVEMENT THROUGHOUT EUROPE TO EMULATE THIS MULTI-NATIONAL APPROACH TO GLOBALIZATION.

They are emphasizing and committing to market-by-market management based upon what the market offers, what the opportunities are, what products are required, and what the best way is to expand the sale of a company's products in a particular market.

One European company, for example, has sent people around the world looking for new sources of specific raw materials. The objective was to lower the cost of materials by shopping the world markets and comparing prices. It's a "win, win" situation. Each local market is helped by getting lower costs and, in the process, becoming more competitive.

We've seen an example where one Japanese supplier was asked to take on, as a specific project, buying a particular material at the best possible price. The result was a significant drop in the cost of that material, far lower than what had been paid earlier.

One more point that's relevant to international development is exemplified by Valco, one of the largest manufacturers of automobile parts in the world. The company is headed by Noel Goutard. He has made enormous changes in a short period of time in Valco's operations. He's a believer in market-by-market selling – in being very close to the local markets before making significant decisions. Goutard has acquired plants in Korea, Brazil, Mexico, and Turkey – not to cut costs, but to be able to establish a stronger foothold in those growing markets. He sees his operations as developing on their own in those four markets by being close to the marketplace and close to the customers.

Goutard fully understands the benefits of this. That's why he wants to keep production ongoing in each place. Goutard says: "We've never seen such changes take place without strong incentives and the incentives are here now. Japanese competition is intense. They are forcing change."

Where did Goutard learn so much about management? "Listening to customers," he says. "Customers can teach you everything you need to know."

Jurgen Strube of BASF brings a farsighted corporate strategy to positioning the company he heads for the next century by building operations in various parts of the world. Mr. Strube has come to symbolize a new breed of German chief executive. These men are internationalists, multi-lingual and well-attuned to separate markets and, most important, customer-oriented – sensitive to the various needs of customers. They no longer think in terms of running their companies in other countries by central command. They have ceded a good deal of control to these separate companies. To arrive at decisions, they depend upon consensus-building, persuasion, and teamwork.

Jurgen Strube says, "We make sure that the heads and hearts of our local colleagues... change. The old ways of doing things no longer works. Sometimes they are completely unsuited for today's global economy. We have to be much more flexible, much more sensitive to local markets and the wants of local customers."

> WORK IN THE MARKETPLACE DEFINES WHERE THERE ARE OPPORTUNITIES TO BUILD SALES AND PROFIT

Why? Because *when the company leader is in the marketplace, he or she is with the customers.* The customers set the tone and pace of what's happening. What they say – in words or by their actions – is a major factor in the decisions the company head will make.

Another great benefit of being in the marketplace is closeness to the competition. There's no question that any president worth the title must be committed to beating competitors as often as possible. And the place to do that is where their products meet – in the marketplace.

Let's look at an example of what can happen when the head of a Vertical Organization encounters fierce competition.

We will not use names, but this is an authentic case

history.

The manager in this example was an experienced soft drink person, with over twenty years of management experience in the field. He was running a large, independent soft drink plant.

The business was profitable when he got the job. He had professionals in all parts of the business for production, marketing, selling, deal-making. The business moved along effectively for the first two years. Things appeared to be in excellent shape; he reported this to top management.

His own management style was to hold weekly review meetings with all of his key people. He expected and received detailed reports from sales, marketing, production, and finance. After making his or her report, everyone present received on-the-spot directions on what to do, what to change, what to do more of. The meeting started at eight and finished by noon.

This leader operated primarily from his office. Any problems that arose were brought to him in his office. He took pride in the fact that his office door was always open.

Then the competition began to get tough: in pricing, in supermarket deals, in value packages. Their prices went up. Their prices went down. Every change depended on the deal-of-the moment. The competition started getting in-aisle displays to promote their ever-changing specials. There was constant movement and constant changes in direction. Every month, the competition had a new and different action which presented our man with a new and different problem.

With so much coming at him, the manager fell into a frame of mind where he was unable to act other than in reaction to his competition.

The competition on the other hand was taking preemptive action after preemptive action. The leader of the competitive company was constantly in stores with his key account people. This competitive leader was determined to win.

And he did.

A good part of the victor's success was the result of what he did personally. He worked the market, he worked the big customers, he fashioned the special deals himself. He knew everything that was going on out in the market.

Meanwhile, the manager who stayed in the office was feeling more than personal pressure. The result of the competition's actions began to be felt where they hurt more than his professional pride: they hurt in sales and profit. His market share dropped, his gross margins dropped. The situation only worsened, and in the end what was sitting on the manager's desk was two years of declining sales and profit performance.

He had been inside his office when he needed to be in the marketplace. He failed to: work with his big customers in their stores; work side-by-side with his people in all the stores; make deals ahead of his competition rather than in response to the deals they were offering. He didn't make a commitment to himself and the company to hold market share and gain market share.

Consider the case of Unifi, an industrial yarn manufacturer. Allen Mebane is Unifi's top manager. "I have got to know my customer's business and differences as well as I know my own."

Mebane emphasizes the importance of getting inside the

customer's mind. He has found a way to meld his interests with those of his customers, understanding that when he helps his customers make money, his own company's profits go up.

For Mebane, this isn't some abstract theory; rather, it's good common sense which he applies every day. Mebane is convinced that he must work inside the customer's business with technical people – those who will use the yarns that he sells. In this way, he can have specific and positive input as to the most effective use of the yarn. Such an evaluation can start with the management level of the customer, but it must go beyond that into the product development section and into the production section of the company. By offering help on an ongoing basis to his customers, Mebane can communicate to them a greater understanding of the quality and versatility of the yarns he sells. Mebane goes so far as to offer his customers the option of having him manufacture yarn to their specifications.

What Allen Mebane does is an example of the highest level of participation in the marketplace.

It requires time and attentiveness. Mebane does it himself, but his example influences other Unifi representatives to work similarly closely with their customers. His work in the market had proved to be invaluable for Unifi.

For a manufacturer of high quality costume jewelry, the business was profitable but growth was slow. The president retired and was replaced by a bright and energetic woman who had only retail experience in jewelry.

She was faced with the problem of choosing designs for the new season. Immediately she left on a two-month trip to twenty of her company's major markets. In each market she met with leading buyers and designers and with leading retailers. She asked questions.

And she listened to the answers.

When she returned she had the equivalent of her own MBA in design, having acquired a grasp of the business that would have taken five years had she chosen to work in the traditional way – mainly in the home office and visiting major conventions and seasonal market shows. This enterprising young woman was able to provide for design and production people precisely the kind of direction they needed. The result was respect from the employees – and a marked increase in the company's profits.

Barnes and Noble Book Stores is a fast-growing company in a business where rapid growth is nearly unheard of.

When competition took on a new form in the shape of the internet, Barnes and Noble paid attention. They are now in direct competition with Amazon.com. But of equal interest is how they let the market dictate changes in their _stores_.

Observing the market closely, Barnes and Noble's top management discovered that people seemed to want more out of a bookstore than in the past. They looked closely at some independent book stores outside metropolitan areas that seemed to combine large size with an intimate feeling. The company tested this idea and it proved out. Now Barnes and Noble's leadership has been opening super stores right and left, based on the concept that a book store should be nearly the same size as a public library, but snug as a den.

This program of expansion came directly out of extensive work by the leadership of Barnes and Noble: they checked the market, talked with customers, observed competitive stores, and finally decided to test in a really big store if what was working for some independents would work there. It did, and that bold move has given them a program for significant expansion.

What do all these successful companies have in common? Only one thing. They know the combination to the safe can be found in the marketplace.

Chapter **14**

JOHNSON & JOHNSON'S
WORLD NETWORK OF CONNECTED
COMPANIES

Johnson & Johnson is a giant among companies. Johnson & Johnson sales exceed $16,000,000,000 and net income exceeds $2,000,000,000. But Johnson & Johnson is no sleeping giant. Johnson & Johnson is similar to ABB, discussed in detail in Chapter 9.

For years, Johnson & Johnson's top management has understood that you can't run a mammoth company from one executive suite. More, they grasped long ago that, even if you set up ten or twenty executive suites, you can't run a company from inside them, either.

Proof of how intelligently Johnson & Johnson is organized: the giant corporation has twenty-eight connected operating companies in the USA alone. Overseas, Johnson & Johnson has distinct operations in over a hundred countries.

Johnson & Johnson refers to these companies as "franchises". But they are effectively Connected Companies. The independent character of the Johnson & Johnson organizational model is a near-perfect match to the Connected Company as I've conceived and created it.

> JOHNSON & JOHNSON HAS IN PLACE THE MOST EFFICIENT AND PRODUCTIVE ORGANIZATION TO DO THE JOB THAT NEEDS TO BE DONE

Johnson & Johnson's companies are all close to the markets and, therefore, to customers, gaining all the resultant benefits. Each franchise has its own president, and he or she spends a good deal of time in the marketplace.

The organizational framework of Johnson & Johnson is based on the broad variety of its products. Much of what Johnson & Johnson sells is marketed abroad as well as in the US; and, Johnson & Johnson has coordinated companies worldwide to handle that market.

Arbitrary control of the individual franchises by a central office is simply not part of how Johnson & Johnson's leadership views their organization.

Johnson & Johnson is always growing. What Johnson & Johnson's leadership has witnessed is the way the way they're organized helps avoid corporate growing pains.

Once the concept of separate but related companies was understood, accepted, and put in place, top management saw that it could rely on this organizational model to ease the way in new markets. There was the opportunity of duplicating the advantages again and again in new territories by setting up additional franchises.

In recent years, Johnson & Johnson has purchased many companies. Most are small operations, purchased because they provide some special product advantages. All offer potential for significant growth.

The broad variety of products in itself argued for an intimate knowledge of the local market. Such knowledge was needed to provide the right focus, in both production and marketing. The many health care products produced and sold by Johnson & Johnson have specific user benefits. In order to focus on the customers for these products and services it was necessary to function at the local level. It was also necessary to understand and comply with local market laws regarding medical products.

Each Johnson & Johnson franchise benefits from the drive and effort produced by the people in charge of running "their own company." The parent company has seen this happen again and again. Throughout this country and in Johnson & Johnson's widespread international operations, the local customers reap their own advantage from the presence of a Johnson & Johnson company. There is more sensitivity to specific needs local customers may have, and there is better and faster service in supplying those needs.

The geographical magnitude of Johnson & Johnson's operation is impressive, as is the broad range of products that are made and sold by Johnson & Johnson franchises. This list of some of the Johnson & Johnson companies gives you an idea of the scope of the business:

Advanced Care Products
Cilag: products for therapeutic use
Ethicon: products for surgeons
Ethicon Endo-Surgery
Greiterag AG :sunscreen products
Iolab : products for ophthalmic market
Janssen Phamaceutica: pharmaceutical products
Clinical Diagnostics: diagnostic test kits
Consumer Products, Inc.: baby care, wound care and
skin care products
LifeScan, Inc.: monitoring systems for people with
diabetes
NcNeil Consumer Products Company: non-prescription
pharmaceuticals
McNeil Specialty Products Company: food and beverage
ingredients
Neutrogena: skin and hair care products
Noramco Inc.: pharmaceuticals, organic chemical and
polymers
Ortho Biotech: products from biotechnological research
Ortho Diagnostic Systems : diagnostic systems to
hospital laboratories
Ortho-McNeil Pharmaceutical: prescription drugs
Penaten :baby toiletries
Personal Products: feminine hygiene and oral care
products
ROC: products for care of sensitive skin
Therakos: photomedical therapy
Vistakon : disposable contact lenses

It would not be possible to market this extraordinary range of products successfully without special knowledge of the various markets for them. That knowledge comes out of the way the operations work in each individual marketplace.

JOHNSON & JOHNSON OPERATES
WITHOUT A MASSIVE BUREAUCRACY

Imagine trying to control and manage all of their companies from a central base. Well, top management at Johnson and Johnson "imagined" it quite a while back, and opted for marketing on a market by market basis.

As a result, Johnson & Johnson avoids all of the entanglements, requirements, and self-serving demands that develop over time in a well-entrenched bureaucracy. It was clear to top management many years ago that such a bureaucracy would strangle the growth and hamper the prosperity of a company with such a broad variety of health care products as diverse as their markets, here and abroad.

I had reports on Johnson & Johnson companies in California, Michigan, New York, and Texas. The objective was to gain a better understanding of their organization. They were very generous about this. Johnson & Johnson product lines are quite different company by company. Indeed, they said that most Johnson & Johnson companies have some products that are exclusive--a significant factor in determining how best to market them.

There is pride in the enterprise. The people in each franchise are deeply involved in every new project. They believe in the beneficial qualities of their products. Employees reported that the sense of "ownership" is important to them, giving them a greater impetus to perform to their utmost. There is a high level of confidence in the products produced and marketed. In short, these are "happy workplaces."

It was plain to me that the leaders of these Johnson & Johnson companies like what they do. Each manager took care to tell about benefits that are enjoyed by each independent Johnson & Johnson company. The level of their interest impressed me. These managers are keenly interested in all the products, the markets, the customers for each product. All project a sense of pride in what they do and what is achieved by "their" franchise.

The financial commitment of Johnson & Johnson is equally impressive. The "home" corporation invests directly in start-up and venture companies in the health care field where promising new technologies are under development. They provide the financial strength needed by each of the operating companies. Financial reporting is done on a continual basis by each of the companies; reports on sales, cost of goods, operating expenses, and operating income are reported by each franchise and to Johnson & Johnson headquarters in New Jersey.

The unified accounting system provides for each company all the accounting information necessary, including balance sheets and operating statements. This is done on a monthly basis. Just consider this technological boon: what could not have been done--or even imagined-- thirty years ago is "business-as-usual" today thanks to the instantaneous communication possible with computers, faxes, telecommunications, etc.

Given its broad product line, Johnson & Johnson could not have thrived – or perhaps even survived – if top management had maintained a typical pyramid organization for the company. In this way, as in numerous other productive ways, Johnson & Johnson was way ahead of the majority of US companies, which have still not broken out of the vise-like vertical mold.

Johnson & Johnson is now in China with the largest pharmaceutical company, China Xian-Jansen Co.! Which should not come as such a surprise when we realize that Johnson & Johnson now operates in forty-eight countries:

Argentina	Indonesia	Scotland
Australia	Ireland	Singapore
Austria	Italy	Slovenia
Belgium	Japan	South Africa
Brazil	Kenya	Spain
Canada	Korea	Sweden
Chile	Malaysia	Switzerland
China	Mexico	Taiwan
Columbia	Morocco	Thailand
Czechoslovakia	Netherlands	Turkey
England	Pakistan	United Arab
France	Panama	Emirates
Germany	Philippines	Venezuela
Greece	Poland	Zambia
Hong Kong	Portugal	Zimbabwe
Hungary	Puerto Rico	
India	Russia	

Frank A. Armstrong

No doubt, others will be added to the list as Johnson &
Johnson continues to expand its operations around the
world.

THE MANY COUNTRIES AND MANY PRODUCT GROUPS
SERVED BY JOHNSON & JOHNSON
COULD ONLY HAVE BEEN PUT IN PLACE
USING THE CONNECTED COMPANY APPROACH.

These "local" companies have been a key factor in the
parent company's growth from sea to shining sea--and
across oceans. Leaders with foresight get a lot of the credit
for that--for making insightful and productive Johnson &
Johnson decisions over the years. What they have put in
place works.

Johnson & Johnson top management is oriented both to
its vast variety of customers and to the people who must
build the individual businesses that serve those customers.
But in the final analysis, Johnson & Johnson's leadership
must look after the interests of their shareholders. The test
of time has confirmed that Johnson & Johnson's
shareholders benefit enormously from the company's
organization into independent franchises.

The Johnson & Johnson credo is impressive. It shows
how the company views its organization and how it
functions in so many countries around the world.

JOHNSON & JOHNSON CREDO

We believe our first responsibility is to the doctors, nurses and patients, to mothers and fathers and all others who use our products and services. In meeting their needs everything we do must be of high quality. We must constantly strive to reduce our costs in order to maintain reasonable prices. Customers' orders must be serviced promptly and accurately. Our suppliers and distributors must have an opportunity to make a fair profit.

We are responsible to our employees, the men and women who work with us throughout the world. Everyone must be considered as an individual. We must respect their dignity and recognize their merit. They must have a sense of security in their jobs. Compensation must be fair and adequate, and working conditions clean, orderly and safe. We must be mindful of ways to help our employees fulfill their family responsibilities. Employees must feel free to make suggestions and complaints. There must be equal opportunity for employment, development and advancement for those qualified. We must provide competent management, and their actions must be just and ethical.

We are responsible to the communities in which we live and work and to the world community as well. We must be good citizens--support good works and charities and bear our fair share of taxes. We must encourage civic improvements and better health and education. We must maintain in good order the property we are privileged to use, protecting the environment and natural resources.

Our final responsibility is to our stockholders. Business must make a sound profit. We must experiment with new

145

ideas. Research must be carried on, innovative programs developed and mistakes paid for. New equipment must be purchased, new facilities provided and new products launched. Reserves must be created to provide for adverse times. When we operate according to these principles, the stockholders should realize a fair return.

It's no surprise that Johnson & Johnson has always been ahead of the pack. Just think: the first surgical sutures were developed and marketed by Johnson & Johnson over a hundred years ago. What is just as amazing, the world famous <u>Band-Aid</u> has changed outside materials and adhesive material dozens of times – always in response to customer needs. That's letting the marketplace lead you – right to leadership in the marketplace.

Chapter **15**

THINKING SMALL IN A BIG WAY

John F. Welch, Jr., who is Chairman of General Electric, has given a great deal of thought to issues of organization. Often, when a big company becomes very big, the organizational framework isn't strong enough to carry the additional weight. One possible solution is to redistribute the weight.

In this interview, Mr. Welch shared his thinking on this subject, and his conclusions specifically as they relate to the need for market by market management.

Why is there such a fascination with small companies? What are you learning from them?

Speed is really the driver that everyone is after. Faster products, faster product cycles to market. Better response time to customers. And there's no question that the smaller one is, and the easier the communication is, the faster one gets. The customer is a much more real person to you, because the customer in a very small company determines what you're going to eat next week. Satisfying customers, getting faster communications, moving with more agility, all these things are easier when one is small. And these are all the characteristics one needs in a fast-moving global environment.

Do you visit with these companies?

I came from a small company. I came from (GE's) plastics company. It was very small, and we ran it like a family grocery store. I would argue that we run GE in a very informal manner. It allows you to get rid of all the ritual and the rigmarole that ties up companies.

Is there a GE business now that is analogous to a small company?

GE Capital has a myriad of activities which replicate that today. I think that our plastics business today is fast-moving and very entrepreneurial. And I think every one of our businesses is infinitely faster than it used to be.

What kinds of businesses within GE moved first?

You normally associate productivity with high growth, rapid technology change, new business. Well, the business that broke the productivity code in GE was lighting. A hundred years old, 2% a year growth. But they got a mind-set around productivity. So they began that launch. And quick response, the ability to get inventory turns very rapidly, that came out of appliances. Not an exciting, fast-moving, revolutionary business. GE Capital clearly has seeded more new businesses of late than anybody else.

Do you bring in small-business people for advisory sessions?

We had Marvin Mann [of IBM spin-off Lexmark]. He came to talk about life in a small company that used to be a division of a big company. And the differences of Lexmark by itself vs. Lexmark in IBM. But I think we all know what we want out of a small company. We know the characteristics; informality, lack of layers, getting close to the customers, making everybody's actions feel like they're important so they [consider] the implications of their actions. Small companies all understand that.

It seems that within our corporate culture, some people who rise to the top might have trouble not giving specific directions, and adapting to this new kind of management.

Don't get me [wrong]. This is not a rudderless ship that we're talking about. The objectives are clearly in focus. We still want to be No. 1 and No. 2 in every business we're in on a global basis. Or we don't want to be in it. So everyone clearly has a focus on what they're doing....It isn't: "Let's come in and have a party here." It's: "Let's gain share, let's get productivity, let's be sure we globalize."

Is there a size or development stage when a small

149

company loses its edge?

As a small company expands rapidly, it runs the risk of setting up structures to manage its growth. And it is the trickiest thing in the world to keep a small company on a growth trajectory and maintain the atmosphere that got them to the dance.

What lessons have you leaned that they would benefit from knowing about?

Managers tend, in the growth cycle, to question in great depth, businesses which are in trouble, but not to question those delivering the goods. [Harvard business school professor] John Kotter, he's got a beautiful diagram. He talks about what happens in high-growth situations and what the organization does. The people start to believe that they are the reasons for the high growth. Then, they organize to manage the high growth. They put in all the bureaucracy, and the bureaucracies start feeding on each other. The customer then gets further and further pushed away.

We have seen any number of companies go up the curve and come down it. Power systems in the early '80s, aircraft engines now. And I take this little thing of Kotter's and every time somebody's behaving this way, I write 'em a little note. And I send this out to them.

Does it then require a different type of manager in the process?

It is very difficult--not impossible, but very difficult--for people who have experienced 10% to 15% to 20%-a-year growth for several years to come to the reality of a changing environment. Now, we've had some successes with this, the most notable one being a locomotive business some years ago where the team did all this and then changed the tires, as we say, while the car was running, because they had to.

Some companies, such as Xerox, have technology ventures where little seedlings bloom. Is there anywhere in GE where you develop really small businesses?

We feel that we can grow within a business, but we are not interested in incubating new businesses. We made a clear, conscious decision - to be argued by some people - that we do not run this incubation laboratory off by itself.

Small-business people say that when they're first starting a business, all of their energy goes in to product development or the technology. But then the business gets to a certain size and they complain that all they do is worry about personnel or financing. And they get away from the things they did to get the business started.

That's all we are; personnel directors. But, we [headquarters managers] accept that role. If we get the right people in the right job, we've won the game. We spend days and days on assessments of people, interviewing people, talking to people. Picking out stock-option recipients. We're dealing with money to allocate to projects and people to allocate to businesses. And we don't do any product development, any pricing, anything like that.

I think you gotta know what your job is. And our jobs aren't picking colors for refrigerators or designing crisper trays.

What has GE learned from Wal-Mart? It's not a small business, but -

It behaves like one, and it's entrepreneurial. Wal-Mart, in my opinion, clearly made a connection between the customer and every employee in Wal-Mart. And they work on that every single day. They just can't stand not filling a customer need. If they're out of blankets in Minneapolis, they've got a computer system that will move the blankets instantaneously to Minneapolis. Or their antifreeze is low in Chicago and high in Kalamazoo, they'll move it. An insatiable desire to make customers love 'em. And tying their personal rewards over the years to doing that, they've seen enormous wealth created at all levels of the store.

We have copied that through QMI, Quick Market Intelligence, in various forms. Our medical business, for example. People say, well, you can't do that in a medical business – heavy equipment, magnetic resonance machines, and stuff like that. But every Friday, their QMI session is aimed at medical today. "Tell us what you need to get that installation in next week." And everybody is on the phone. The plant manager, the engineering manager, all the head guys. That's our adaptation of a Wal-Mart thing.

You mentioned expanding the reward system from 300 to 14,000 employees?

No, about 8,000, 9,000, something like that.

Is that one of the ways small companies energize their employees?

You should see the pulse of this place when the stock hits 100. The building almost shakes. Because lots of people, at all levels, have options.

How do you decide to give someone a stock option?

Some people believe in giving broad stock options to all employees. We like to differentiate. We have all kinds of guidelines. [For example,] 50 percent of them have to be less than 10 years in the company. We mix it up. So that people aren't just handing it out as a routine thing.

Another small-company thing here is that I meet once a quarter with all the purchasing people. And they're all in telling their vignettes about what they're doing too. We meet with all the sales managers once a quarter. So they're sharing best practices. So doing that, we end up being right down in the trenches on a lot of details. That's a small-company attribute, I think.

There's a flip side to it, though. There are a lot of small-business people worrying about whether their payroll checks are going to bounce who would love to have GE's financial muscle. So bigness gives you

153

something.

We can stay in businesses that other people had to leave because they couldn't hang in there. Your training skills and strengths are bigger and better. But the thing that we're all trying to do - and I don't think GE's any different than anybody else - we're desperately trying to combine the best of both. This interview was reported in <u>Business Week</u> by Tim Smart and Judith Dobrzynski.

Afterword

MAYBE YOU SHOULD TRY IT

It can be productive for any business to add a new and different source of sales and profit growth. That's what establishing a Connected Company offers you.

This book contains most of the practical information that you would need to start a Connected Company. I wrote this book as a "work manual." As a practical manual, this book covers each part of the actions needed to set up a Connected Company. They aren't complicated or expensive. In the process you will be considering various markets that have the potential for new growth. It is easy if you start with just one market. Prove that it works and then go on to another – and another.

I started Monarch's first Connected Company in the Southwest where there was a need for growth and a number of promising sales opportunities. It worked. We went on to expand to the West Coast and then overseas.

You can get started in an economical and easy way by making good use of various specialists already in your own company. The treasurer can plan the use of capital. The internal auditors can use the methods for operating control as defined in Chapter 7. You can select the person to run your new U.S. company from inside your own work force-- probably someone in sales but he or she could be from any other part of the company. The key requirement for the manager you choose is that person's drive and capability to build a new business. It would be difficult to overstate the need for care in this selection process. The right leader, working on his own, will help to confirm the practical qualities of the entire plan.

The leader's first job will be to help choose the group of people to set up the Connected Company. Picking the right market to start is equally important.

Everything you do should reflect your business smarts. Be sure you have the right market and the right products and the right leader and the right staff to run--and build--the business. There is a need to stay close enough to the new company so you can follow its progress closely. That will insure that costs are kept down and risk kept to a minimum.

The upside is virtually limitless.

Monarch's first Connected Company was productive in the first year. And that was only the start of what establishing Connected Companies did for our business.

Chances are, they can do as much for yours.

I wish you good fortune.

Frank A. Armstrong

ABOUT THE AUTHOR

Frank A. Armstrong

Former management board chairman of advertising giant, McCann-Erickson, Frank had responsibility for the accounts of Coca Cola, Owens Fiberglass, Goodyear International, and Deering Millikin.

In 1972, Frank assumed the helm of a small, soft-drink bottler, the Moxie Company. Moxies's annual sales were then less than $1 million. By 1981, Frank propelled Moxie's annual sales to more than $60 million.

Frank and his son, Mark, acquired the Monarch Company in 1985. Incorporating the aggressive sales, marketing, and product development axioms found in *The Connected Company*, Monarch grew exponentially. The product line now includes *Dad's Root Beer, Bubble Up, NuGrape* and more than 25 other brands.

The Armstrongs catapulted sales and multiplied Monarch's structure to more than 600 U.S. and international franchisees.

Instrumental in this growth was the developed philosophy now found in *The Connected Company.*

In 1996, Frank was inducted into the Beverage World Hall of Fame. Frank Armstrong has authored four other business management books. He attended Rutgers and Princeton universities and has a degree in economics.